This guide is one of the outcomes of the DAP Health Hub
project, funded under the Technology Strategy Board's Assisted
Living Innovation Platform.
The intellectual property and copyright are owned by the Royal
Institute of British Architects.
The right of the Royal Institute of British Architects to be
identified as the author of this work has been asserted in
accordance with the Copyright, Designs and Patents Act 1988
Sections 77 and 78.

ISBN 9781859464236

9 781859 464236

Acknowledgements

This work was part funded by The Technology Strategy Board.

Contributions to the work were made by the following:

BRE - Ranjit Bassi, Keith Quillin
3DReid Research - Paul Warner, David Maher
RIBA - Keith Snook, Luis Belmonte

Support and technical assistance was provided by an industry
steering group including:

Microsoft
Cisco
Centri Health
Telemedic
Herewood College
F.A.S.T
Bournemouth Council
Willmott Dixon
Sasie

Advice as part of the document was provided by:

HOIP
ITSupport
The Technology Strategy Board

Additional assistance in setting up the guide has been provided
by Stuart Wheeler and Joe Shaw at 3DReid.

The guide is one of the outcomes of the DAP Health Hub project,
funded under the Technology Strategy Board's Assisted Living
Innovation Platform.

Preface

Wired Up

The idea that people can support themselves longer by the assistance of technical devices is now reality. From simple self care systems to tele-systems that help with disability or illness require different degrees of reliability in their performance criteria.

Data is transmitted by both wired and wireless systems but interoperability between appliances with proprietary wireless systems is convenient and very likely to become more sophisticated in the future. Unfortunately wireless systems are prone to interference and commonly do not transmit data as safely as wired systems. So today there is a necessary interface between systems that are wired and those that are wireless.

Mobile phones are now becoming information systems that will in the future interface with the home in many more ways than is possible today. Currently end to end connection is provided by a plethora of part wired and part wireless systems.

Interfaces and interoperability between systems and appliances are at the heart of this research and references to more detailed information are included. Space standards, ergonomic data and the consideration of how to support living at home whilst being less able-bodied are also included in the guide.

Information is applicable to new build homes but there is in section five an emphasis on the conversion of existing housing stock into homes suitable for assisted living as this is seen as the bigger market. The difficulties with existing housing stocks are usually borne out of material that could not possibly have been considered as a problem when they were built. Solutions such as the Faraday Cage effect that steel reinforcement in concrete structures provides. Interference from ducted water systems and the simple block in transmission from foil backed or metal mesh plasterwork are common problems.

Each section in the handbook refers to more detailed guidance from appropriate regulators or relevant bodies.

In the foreseeable future the goal for assisted living is that all essential equipment in the home is connected to a form of hub that can receive and transmit information to assist people to live at home whatever their health condition (apart from critical).

White goods and other home appliances and services will become more and more intelligent. They will interoperate (see definitions below on interoperability and software systems), and know if they have been 'left on' too long. Fridges will know which products need replacing. This information will be transmitted beyond the home to receivers anywhere.

Interoperability - where different application functions are able to use shared information in a consistent way. This requires interworking as a building block as well as co-existence, and adds business rules, processes and security provisions that enable applications to be joined together; e.g a home wireless security system being controlled and monitored remotely using a seperate web application, sending alerts to the owners' mobile phone or TV set. The benefit is that applications can interact with each other and create greater efficiences by sharing resources across multiple systems. Interoperability should also lead to improved ease of use, better human factor capability, greater choice, international economies of scale and hence lower unit costs. 1.

So the benefits of being connected will range from pure convenience to the transmission of critical health data.

Hub data and operation will be as important as electricity, gas and water supply are today.

Assisted living technology today is implemented in hardware. Full software radio, would allow for the development of extremely flexible devices, whose capabilities can be updated in real time using over the air updates. Assisted living devices that are software rather than hardware based could be a radical departure for assisted living, but realistically are several years away. 2.

This guide forms part of the Assisted Living research programme, ALIP 1. Brief details of this research are as follows.

Health Hub Project

This ALIP1 project led by the DAP Consortium has delivered the following significant outputs:

The Vision
A DVD Demonstrator Tool illustrating 6 user-based scenarios showcasing the tangible, life enhancing benefits that assisted living support services enabled by integrated digital communications can deliver for users, carers, their families and friends.

Design Principles
A strategic Framework and set of design principles to support the development of integrated user focused assisted living services enabled through the application of open access standards, to provide anywhere, anytime, any medium scalable and upgradable services.

Demonstration of integrated assisted living solutions
An overview of the demonstration of a model of user focused assisted living services based on digital integration. The demonstration has established the scope for seamless, scalable and upgradable real time connection between sensors, personal data records and communication to the user and health and social service professionals.

RIBA/BRE Design Guide
A unique design guide aimed at architects and other design professionals on the appropriate design of new and refurbished homes to create a safe and comfortable internal environment for those living with long term chronic conditions and whose wellbeing and quality of life can be better supported by assisted living solutions.

Requirements for Large Scale Testing
The definition of a set of requirements that systems can be tested against in relation to design, manufacture and supply to market.

Exploitation and future development –
A set of strategies for technical and market development by partner organisations.

Information on the DAP ALIP1 Project along with downloads of the project outputs is available on the DAP website: www.dapforum.org

Please refer to the Acknowledgements for the DAP ALIP1 Project Partners.

Digital connection will become increasingly important for health-care and other needs particularly for the elderly. Today in the UK 97% of households have a TV and the immediate solutions for digital inclusion utilise this friendly technology for the elderly to use. As a more technical literate generation get older they will be more familiar with a partially virtual tele-care world and future equipment that goes with this world.

Virtual health vaults will be commonplace and keeping records (both personal and professional), providing help and reminders by means of tele data/medicine/information will be normal activity.

At the end of the guide there is the opportunity to record and update examples of newly finished projects, future research proposals and new technical innovation.

1, 2.
G. Worsley - Assisted living Innovation Platform - Standards, Interoperability and Broadband.

Contents

Introduction

Introduction

In common with most developed countries, the United Kingdom's population is ageing rapidly. In 20 years time, one third of Britons will be aged 60 or more, with many other European countries in a similar position. Whilst our increasing longevity is something to celebrate, the economic, social and political implications are very significant. For example, as populations age, the incidence of chronic disease rises dramatically. These conditions account for up to 80% of total healthcare spending in the UK not to mention the impacts for the individuals, families and communities concerned. The changing demographic means that traditional arrangements for supporting those with long term conditions will not be sustainable even in the medium term. Neither are they desirable for the large majority of people, who want - and increasingly expect – to maintain their chosen lifestyles.

The (physical) built environment, and the way in which it is designed and adapted to meet the needs of people with different levels of mobility and capability, and throughout their life is clearly a key factor if people are to be supported to remain in their homes for as long as possible. It is not just a passive element when it comes to assistive living; it is a key part of the delivery both socially, digitally and physically. However, it is also important that people do not become prisoners in their own homes; mobile devices and services that can support users in managing conditions outside the home are needed. These will need to operate seamlessly with home-based solutions.

This document provides guidance to those who may have to take decisions on the appropriate design, specification, construction and adaptation of 'assisted living enabled' buildings. This group of people will include developers, designers, builders, various consultants, health care workers, designers of health care equipment and the general public who are involved in caring for the elderly or less able. However considering the wide ranging scope of the document references are made throughout to other more detailed sources of knowledge regarding both physical, technical and tele-care data. The majority of information in the guide relates to the built environment.

The guide builds on:

Lifetime Homes principles and existing codes and standards.

Best practice in the design of smart homes.

Evolving assisted living concepts arising from recent developments in technology and associated services.

Suggested areas for future research.

The first section addresses building fabric and space issues, the second looks at approaches to the integration of digital infrastructure into homes and small communities such as residential blocks.

What is assisted living?

The "Assisted Living" agenda includes approaches, services, solutions, capabilities and related technologies which:

Help elderly people, and those with chronic conditions to live active, independent and dignified lives with maximum personal control for the individual citizen or patient.

Help minimise the exacerbation of chronic conditions and consequent effects.

Help extend individuals' participation in their communities, in work, leisure and community activities.

Help support the capacity and effectiveness of professional and voluntary care providers to meet the needs of those with chronic conditions, whilst also meeting carers own needs.

Enable support to be provided in effective, scalable and affordable ways.

Stimulate new thinking and new models of support based on contemporary and emerging technologies.

Help the designers and providers of relevant built environments to enable each of the above.

These considerations apply to people of all ages, whilst recognising that the large majority of those who have chronic conditions are also older citizens. The assisted living agenda therefore seeks to promote truly inclusive design thinking to all environments, practices, services and products.

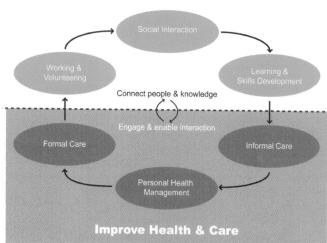

Critical Independencies | Benefits from integrated digital communication technologies | Underpinned by high-speed broadband connectivity | Open architectures for standards

Figure 1.1 below, shows six assisted living 'focus areas' which contribute to:

The direct improvement in healthcare and extending participation.

The focus areas are summarised in the following sections. More details are included in the DAP document 'A framework for assisted living'.

1. Improve Health and Care

Personal Health Management
Personal health management involves empowering the individual to maintain their own well-being through improved knowledge about their existing long-term condition(s) or through general health promotion as a preventative approach. It will typically be targeted at the more able bodied person who purchases personal health systems out of pocket to better manage his or her own health.

Formal Care
In the home or in a community setting, formal care, i.e. that which is usually provided by a health or care professional, is becoming an increasing strain on Local Authorities, NHS Trusts and others. Supplementing these services through Assisted Living technology helps to scale the delivery of formal care and

make it more sustainable for the provider. Terms often used to refer to different types of formal care service are listed overleaf.

Informal Care
Informal care extends the boundaries of care to families, volunteers, charities and other carer groups. This extends the reach of Assisted Living solutions beyond that of the patient's home, perhaps to the caregiver's home or even when on the move. Informal carers provide the greatest part of care for older people in almost all European countries. If we are to continue to rely on this army of older informal carers we need to support them with appropriate information, safety nets and emotional support, as well as the services to help them fulfil their caring roles, and live the other parts of their lives.

2. Extending participation

Working and Volunteering
A very high proportion of people with chronic conditions – many of whom are well beyond traditional retirement age - are active and very able. Mental and physical stimulation promotes wellbeing, hence helps to minimise further health, social and economic challenges. Work to support those with chronic conditions and provide environments for them to live in should therefore seek to maximise their opportunity to participate in active work-paid or not - for as long as practical and in ways which suit their needs and situation. The same is equally true for those who care for family members and friends with more serious conditions: they too need the flexibility and enablement to do so, and to live active lives outside of caring, constrained as little as possible by where they are or when they are in a position to do so.

Social Interaction
Whilst the ability to connect places, knowledge and things in effective ways has reached unprecedented levels, connecting people remains the most compelling and personal proposition of all. Today's modes of communication enable new ways to interact with family and friends, service providers and communities, that are quick, efficient and user friendly. All these possibilities, and the social enrichment they can bring, make the enablement of them another central part of a comprehensive Assisted Living strategy. Improving social interaction like this promotes well-being by stimulating and engaging, avoiding disenfranchisement, and promoting connection with the wider community and society in general.

Learning & Skills Development
Life-long learning has value on several levels, for those with chronic conditions themselves, the communities around them, and for all related providers who serve or otherwise interact with them. As leading academic entities, employers and millions of individuals have found, integrated digital communications – if suitably connected - open up a multitude of opportunities to invigorate and improve the whole learning and skills development process, including planning, design, delivery, access, reach, participation, effectiveness, efficiency, assessment and continuous improvement.

Assistive technology has the potential to improve the quality of life, well-being and autonomy of older people and those with long term conditions, enabling them to remain in their homes for as long as possible.

Formal care terminology

TeleCare
The Telecare Services Association defines Telecare as:
"A service which provides people who are usually elderly or vulnerable with the support to help them lead independent lifestyles. Telecare equipment makes it possible for them to call for help and assistance when needed".

Telecare includes systems designed to actually deliver "care" to people without necessarily making direct reference to their health. For example:

A pendant alarm enables someone with some level of incapacity to access "care" that may alleviate some immediate need, typically by contacting help quickly, but with no specific reference to their particular condition.

An expert system that would alert help if an elderly or vulnerable person falls over in the night, or if a blind person trips in the street or if a dementia patient gets disorientated or lost.

Currently UK telecare services support mainly elderly and vulnerable people to live independently in their own home through the use of sensors. Telecare provides 24 hour monitoring of an individual, ensuring an alert is raised if the sensor detects any problems. If a Telecare sensor activates in an individuals home an alert is automatically raised to a 24 hour response centre who will maintain contact with the user to check on their safety and arrange the appropriate support by contacting a family member, mobile warden or emergency service. The response centre has access to information on the service user and can identify what sensor in the home has activated to ensure the appropriate responses are arranged promptly. Service is currently paid for by the social services departments in the UK.

TeleHealth
The UK Department of Health define telehealth as:

"The remote exchange of physiological data between a patient at home and medical staff at hospital to assist in diagnosis and monitoring. Amongst other things it comprises home units to measure and monitor temperature, blood pressure and other vital signs for clinical review at a remote location (for example, a hospital site) using phone lines or wireless technology."

Systems in this category make use of Information and communications technology to assist a person to manage their own health conditions directly. Typically they would include the measurement of certain parameters in a long-term condition that would allow a patient to monitor their state of health and adjust their care regime themselves. Measurements made in this category may not necessarily have the accuracy typically taken by medical professionals but would be accurate enough to be considered "Health Indicators", allowing the general trend to be observed and to trigger more professional help should a condition deteriorate.

TeleHealth systems may typically be used by patients with long-term but stable conditions, and by people recovering normally at home from illness or operations. But they may also be useful to people without known conditions but who are interested to manage their normal fitness (in order to adjust a fitness regime) or their ageing process obtaining reassurance that early changes in health indicators can alert them to seek medical help before more serious symptoms occur. In this respect, TeleHealth systems may be "elective" for fitness or normal ageing purposes, and "prescriptive" for those with diagnosed conditions.

TeleMedicine
The UK Department of Health defines telemedicine as:

"the use of medical information exchanged from one site to another via electronic communications to improve patients' health status. This typically involves remote consultations with specialists to supports care delivery as well as health education and the transfer of medical data."

Systems under the label TeleMedicine are designed to be used by medical professionals in conjunction with patients. In this category, the measurements taken by systems are designed to be of sufficient quality to be used for diagnostic purposes. The key factors here are:

Expert availability: TeleMedicine would normally at some stage involve the direct participation of a medical professional, or in some controlled cases, expert software systems under the supervision of medical professionals.

Location: the patient no longer has to be in a clinical environment for diagnostic quality measurements to be taken.

Remote links: the medical professionals do not have to be in the same location as the patient.

Confidence: medical professionals need to be able to have confidence that the information provided allows them to take serious decisions about prescribing treatment.

Hospital at Home / Hospice at Home
Hospital at Home and Hospice at Home represent more serious levels of care that allow patients to be treated in their home settings as if they were in a hospital or hospice. Such care regimes necessarily involve higher quality systems and professional involvement, but may still be cost-effective (because of the higher costs of providing such services in hospitals) as well as preferred by patients (who may be more comfortable in their home). Many of the systems provided by TeleCare, TeleHealth and TeleMedicine could find a place in Hospital-at-Home and Hospice-at-Home settings.

The research will cover current guidance and future recommendations for the design of Assisted Living accommodation for both new and existing housing stock within the UK. Retrofitting existing housing is important for two main reasons. Existing stock far exceeds new build quantities. Guidance for existing stock may be, in part, different from that for an ideal new build model.

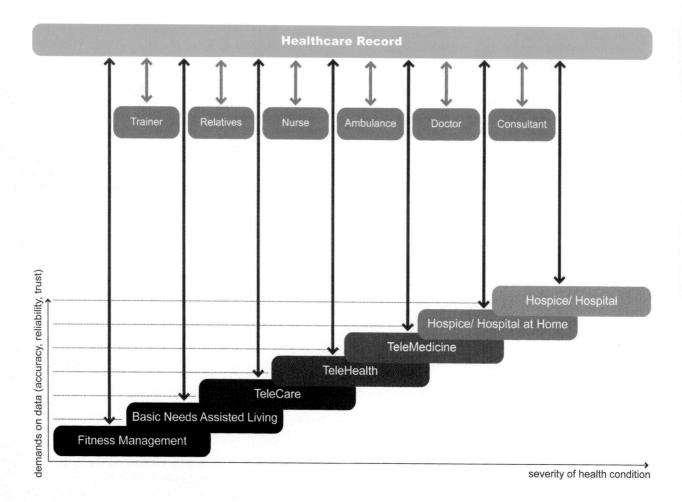

Figure 1.2
Demands on data vs severity of health condition - BRE

1. Housing Standards Matrix

Housing Standards Matrix

The following lists common standards and guidance for housing, and the table overleaf shows a matrix of the most common standards grouped into types.

Planning Policy Statements 1 & 3
Planning Policy Statements 1 (Sustainable Development) & 3 (Housing) provide the national policy framework for housing delivery and creating sustainable communities. Planning Authority Supplementary Planning Documents offer policy guidance on housing, urban design and sustainability.

Homes & Communities Agency (HCA)
The Homes and Communities Agency (HCA) is the non-departmental public body that funds new affordable housing in England. It was established by the Housing and Regeneration Act 2008 as one of the successor bodies to the Housing Corporation, and became operational on 1 December 2008.

The HCA was developed following the amalgamation to bring together the investment functions of the Housing Corporation, English Partnerships and parts of the Department for Communities and Local Government to form a new unified housing and regeneration agency. It would also incorporate the functions of the Academy for Sustainable Communities and the government's advisory team for large applications. The HCA is also the publisher of further design guidance on Urban Design Compendium and Car Parking.

Housing Quality Indicator
Housing Quality Indicators (HQIs) measure the quality of housing schemes funded through the National Affordable Housing Programme (NAHP).

The HCA use the Housing Quality Indicator system as an assessment tool deciding on suitable funding, scoring potential developments on dwelling size, layouts, services and site development.

Lifetime Homes
The Lifetime Homes standard is a series of sixteen design criteria intended to make homes more easily adaptable for lifetime use. The concept was initially developed in 1991 by the Joseph Rowntree Foundation and Habinteg Housing Association. Lifetime Homes is encouraged by the HCA and maybe required by local planning authorities depending on the authority and development. Lifetime Homes is influential towards the Code for Sustainable Homes. Further technical support on Lifetime Homes is provided by Habinteg.

A revised edition of Lifetime Homes was published in July 2010 in response to a consultation, introduced to achieve a higher level of practicability for volume developers in meeting the requirements of the Code for Sustainable Homes.

Code for Sustainable Homes
The Code for Sustainable Homes is an environmental impact rating system for housing in England & Wales, setting new standards for energy efficiency, with assessments undertaken by the Building Research Establishment (BRE). In 2010 Code level 3 compliance is mandatory for public and private sector new-build residences, including flats and houses. A funding requirement will be applicable in 2012 by the HCA to achieve Level 4.

Building for Life
Building for Life is a tool for assessing the design quality of homes and neighbourhoods in England. It was developed by the Commission for Architecture and the Built Environment (CABE), with partners the Home Builders Federation, the Civic Trust and Design for Homes.

The Building for Life tool comprises 20 areas of criteria to assess the design quality of new housing developments. The approach embodied by the criteria is based on urban design principles and quality issues set out on national Planning Policies. The criteria also relate to other standards for housing design, including the BREEAM EcoHomes standard, the Code for Sustainable Homes Lifetime Homes and Secured by Design.

Mayor of London Housing Space Standards
All housing built on LDA land is expected to meet these standards. The standards will also start to be applied to housing schemes applying for funding from the London Homes and Communities Agency (HCA). The guide promotes better neighbourhoods, high environmental standards, better accessibility and better design in new publicly-funded housing. This includes new minimum standards for the amount of floor space and private outdoor space, as well as guidance on natural light and ceiling heights. The guide identifies key areas which have an important effect on the quality of design during the initial stages of a development.

Refer to Chapter 4 for Space Standards from the London Housing Space Standards.

Design For Access 2
Manchester City Council's Design For Access 2 disability standard which goes beyond Building Regulations & Lifetime Homes standards, enforced through Planning.

Further detailed information regarding Design for Access 2 is covered in Chapter 3 Access.

Modern Methods of Construction
The Modern Methods of Construction (MMC) focuses on building products and system construction innovations and off-site manufactured modern methods of construction. The range of construction systems ranges from developments in timber-frame, steel-frame, pre-cast concrete systems, structural insulated panel systems (SIPS), etc, Affordable Housing, ECO Homes, Sustainable Buildings, Renewable and Sustainable Energy and is encouraged by HCA for funding schemes.

National House Building Council (NHBC)
On new builds the NHBC inspector carries out a series of "Key stage" inspections. This is to ensure the properties are built to the standards of both the NHBC and the Council of Mortgage Lenders (CML). The key stage are Foundations, drainage, superstructure i.e. brickwork etc, pre-plaster and pre-handover to the customer.

National Housing Federation (NHF)
The National Housing Federation (NHF) is the umbrella organisation for social housing providers in the UK, publishing good practice guides such as 'Standards & Quality in Development' and 'Accommodating Diversity' among other specialist guidance publications.

BS 8300:2009
British Standards BS 8300:2009 Design of buildings and their approaches to meet the needs of disabled people Code of Practice. The British Standard applies to accessible design of buildings both internally and externally.

Wheelchair Housing Design Guide
'Wheelchair Housing Design Guide' published by Habinteg Housing Association. Industry standard reference for good practice guidance on accessible housing design.

Carbonlite Programme

The Carbonlite Programme - an AECB (Association for Environmentally Conscious Building), initiative providing guidance and information for the development of low-energy buildings covering both domestic and non-domestic buildings. The programme offers a building assessments scheme and 'step by step' guides on design and construction.

Passivhaus

Passivhaus is the leading international low energy, design standard developed in Germany. The standard is administered in the UK by the BRE. The standard covers a variety of building typologies from houses, schools and offices.

CABE

The Commission for Architecture and the Built Environment (CABE) is an executive non-departmental body of the UK government. CABE is the government's advisor on architecture, urban design and public space in England. CABE's main function is design review - expert independent assessments of buildings. CABE's design review panel consists of around 40 expert advisors drawn from England's architectural, built environment and creative community. In addition to the design review assessments, CABE also publish guidance documentation such as 'Homes for Old Age – Independent living by design'.

Manual for Streets

The Manual for Streets provides guidance for practitioners involved in the planning, design, provision and approval of new streets, and modifications to existing ones. It aims to increase the quality of life through good design which creates more people-oriented streets. Although the detailed guidance in the document applies mainly to residential streets, the overall design principles apply to all streets within urban areas.

Housing Corporation Standards

The Housing Corporation Standards was disbanded in 2008 with the service transferred into two separate organisations: The Tenants Services Authority (TSA), responsible for social tenants and the Homes & Communities Agency (HCA), responsible for new housing.

The HCA have worked closely with the Mayor of London to develop the London Housing Standards. In addition they have commissioned a panel to gather good practice from across Europe and put together new and creative proposals to help put older people at the forefront of housing: Housing our Population Panel for Innovation (HAPPI).

Robust Details

Robust details provides guidance on materials and construction details for the separating wall/floor and its key interfaces with other elements to comply with Building Regulations Part E: Resistance to Passage of Sound.

Secured by Design

Secured by Design is focused on crime prevention at the design, layout and construction stages of homes and commercial premises and promotes the use of security standards for a wide range of applications and products. Secure by Design is a requirement for HCA funded schemes and is an additional scoring mechanism towards CfSH. SBD is also required by Local Planning Authorities.

Type of Standard	Legal		Conditional		Voluntary	
	National (Building Regs)	Local (Planning)	Funding (HCA)	Insurance	Commercial	Best Practice
Space/ Layout	Part B	London Housing Design Guide	Housing Quality Indicators			The Good Loo Guide - CAE
Accessibility	Part M	Design for Access 2 (Manchester City Council)	Lifetime Homes			BS8300 2009 Wheelchair Housing Design Guide
Sustainability	Parts J, L	Supplementary Planning Documents	Code for Sustainibility Homes (CforSH)			(CforSH) Carbonlite Programme, Passivhaus
Construction / Technical	Parts A-H, N, P		Secured By Design, Modern Methods of Construction	National House Building Council etc.	Robust Details	BRE
Urban Design	Planning Policy Statements 1&3	Supplementary Planning Documents	Building For Life, Secured by Design			HCA, CABE, Manual for Streets, CAE Accessible Ironmongery

Table 1.1
Housing Standards Matrix

2. Ergonomic
Development & Data

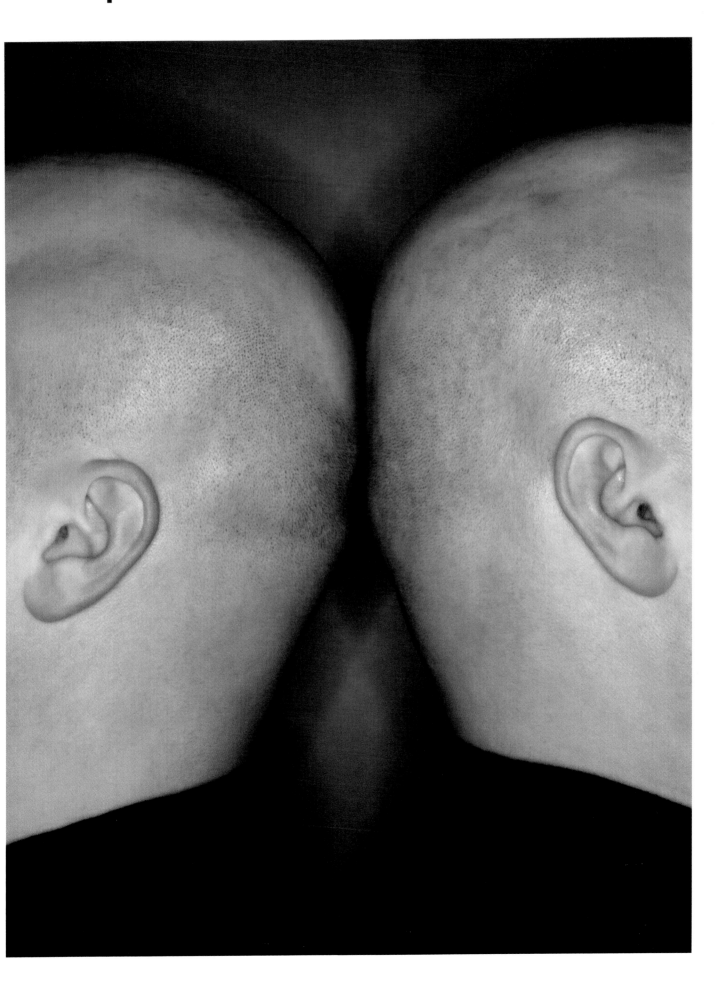

Anthropometric Data

Introduction

The average person does not exist; when you take the average of all body dimensions of a certain group you will end up with a description of a person that does not exist. It is very rare that an individual person has multiple body dimensions that are average for a population. However, the average value of one dimension, like stature, does exist and makes sense.

Anthropometry is the scientific study of measurements of the human body. Anthropometric data can be a valuable source of information when designing products, buildings and spaces. Not only when spatial dimensions have to be determined, but also in the early stages for the development of ideas.

This shows that although anthropometry can provide designers with statistical information about the dimensions of the human body, this available information can never be directly translated to product dimensions. How anthropometric information can be used depends on the specific situation, the nature and complexity of the design problem. The decision on what techniques to use in a design process can depend on even more factors like available data, time and money. A designer should use the appropriate techniques to make sure that design decisions based on anthropometric data are valid.

The results that are presented are categorized according to the amount of dimensions that have been taken into account, allowing for the basic development areas and environments. Less dimensions can mean easier interpretation of data, but also more abstraction in comparison to the real situation.

Ergonomic development

The anthropometric data diagrams are derived from two sources. One is Henry Dreyfuss Associates' *The Measure of Man and Woman - Human Factors in Design*, published in 1993. The other is the second edition of Stephen Pheasant's 'Bodyspace', sub-titled Anthropometry, Ergonomics and the Design of Work, published in 1998.

Henry Dreyfuss's 1993 book is the updated sequel to his 1960 landmark book, *The Measure of Man*.

During World War II he was commissioned by the US Department of Defence to develop human engineering standards for the design of military equipment. He undertook a survey of a large sample of adult males in military service or suited for it. The findings informed the anthropometric diagrams in the 1960 book.

In the 1976 edition of *Designing for the Disabled*, the anthropometric diagrams, derived from Dreyfuss's 1960 book, the height of building fixtures that were being drafted was that the 5th percentile did not sensibly represent short people, and nor did the 95th represent tall people. That might have been predicted, owing to short and tall men having been disregarded for the purpose of Dreyfuss's 1940s project on specific equipment for military personnel.

One of the concerns was that in the 1993 book the 50th percentile for the stature of adult men continued to be shown at 1755mm as it had been in the 1960 book, this being a measure that had come from a survey made in the 1940s.

Stephen Pheasant's Data

Adult men in Britain in the twenty-first century, an average height of 1755mm (5ft 9 in) could be an underestimate.

For British adults ages 19 to 65 the Pheasant estimate for the 50th percentile measure of the stature of men is 1740mm. This is with unshod feet; with 25mm added for the kind of everyday

	Men Percentiles		
	5th	50th	95th
Aged 19-65	1625	1740	1855
Aged 65-85	1575	1685	1790
Elderly People	1515	1640	1765

Table 2.1
Male Statures - *Metric Handbook, Planning and Design data*

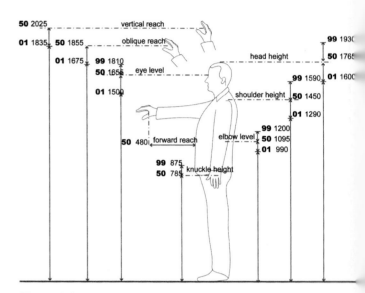

Figure 2.1
Able bodied men age 18-60
Metric Handbook, Planning and Design data

	Women Percentiles		
	5th	50th	95th
Aged 19-65	1505	1610	1710
Aged 65-85	1475	1570	1670
Elderly People	1400	1515	1630

Table 2.2
Female Statures - *Metric Handbook, Planning and Design data*

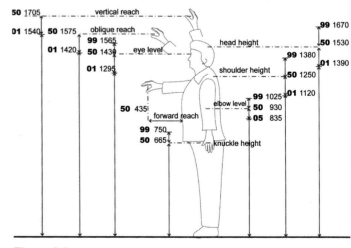

Figure 2.2
Elderly women age 60+
Metric Handbook, Planning and Design data

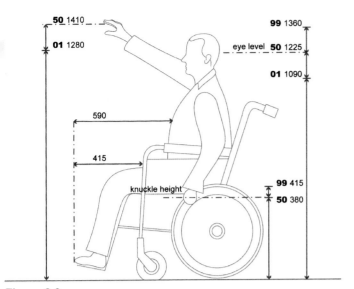

Figure 2.3
Wheelchair user, man, with unimpaired upper limbs
Metric Handbook, Planning and Design data

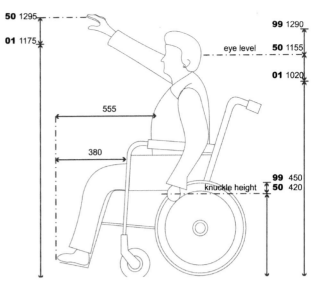

Figure 2.4
Wheelchair user, woman, with unimpaired upper limbs
Metric Handbook, Planning and Design data

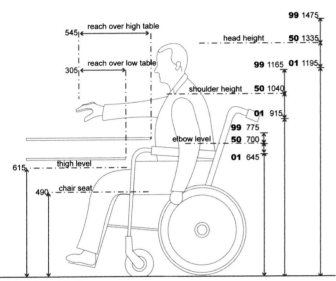

Figure 2.5
Wheelchair user, man, with unimpaired upper limbs
Metric Handbook, Planning and Design data

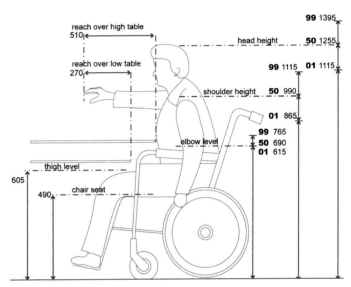

Figure 2.6
Wheelchair user, woman, with unimpaired upper limbs
Metric Handbook, Planning and Design data

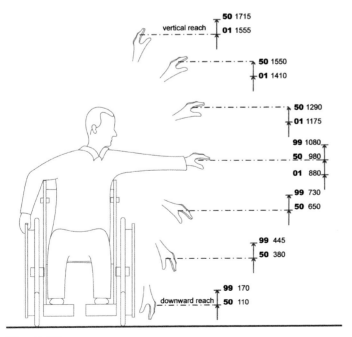

Figure 2.7
Wheelchair user, man, with unimpaired upper limbs
Metric Handbook, Planning and Design data

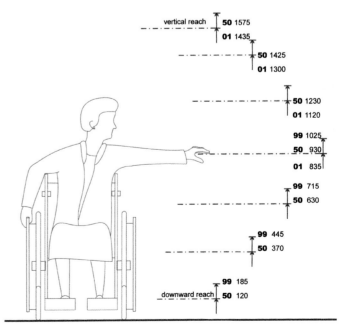

Figure 2.8
Wheelchair user, woman, with unimpaired upper limbs
Metric Handbook, Planning and Design data

23

shoes that men wear, this becomes 1765mm (5ft 9 ½ in) in place of Dreyfuss's 1755mm.

For the stature of the women corresponding 50th percentile Pheasant measure is 1610mm; with 10mm flat shoes the average height of women becomes 1620mm and with 100mm high-heel shoes 1710mm. Average heel height is assumed to be 40mm, giving an average height of 1650mm (5ft 5in) in place of Dreyfuss's 1625mm (5ft 4in).

In recording anthropometric data, head height is the key item, and average measures of other bodily characteristics may not have equally neat statistical correspondences. Diversity is the rule. As people become older they diminish in size and during adult life bodily changes occur within any individual and among groups of comparable individuals. People in different geographical areas, types of employment or social groups develop in different ways, and among people in different ethnic groups there are distinctively different bodily characteristics.

Ergonomic Information

People tend to shrink slightly with age. (On average a change of 10 cm – see table below.) More significantly, the body tends to be less flexible in regard to adapting to dimensionally unfavourable situations.

It is therefore important that design allows for the safe and comfortable access, movement and activity of elderly people within the limits of their height, movement & reach constraints. Statures (mm) for Britons in various age groups:

The Universal Design Pyramid

In Row 1 at the foot of the eight-level pyramid are fit agile people.

In Row 2 are the generality of normal adult able-bodied people, while not being athletic.

Scoring as at Pointer A, no small children in Rows 1 and 2.

The people in Row 3 are in the main also normal able-bodied people.

When Row 3 attempt to use public toilets they are regularly subjected to architectural discrimination because the number of wcs provided for them is typically less than half the number of urinals and wcs that men are given.

In row 4 are elderly people, perhaps going around with a walking stick, people with infants in pushchairs.

In row 5 are ambulant people who have disabilities.

Standing	Men Percentilles			Women Percentilles		
	5th	50th	95th	5th	50th	95th
1 Stature	1575	1685	1790	1475	1570	1670
2 Eye Height	1470	1575	1685	1375	1475	1570
3 Shoulder Height	1280	1380	1480	1190	1280	1375
4 Elbow Height	975	895	975	740	810	875
5 Hand (knuckle) Height	670	730	795	645	705	760
6 Reach upwards	1840	1965	2090	1725	1835	1950
Sitting						
7 Height above seat level	815	875	930	750	815	885
8 Eye height above seat level	705	760	815	645	710	770
9 Shoulder height above seat level	520	570	625	475	535	590
10 Length from elbow to fingertip	425	460	490	390	420	450
11 Elbow above seat level	175	220	270	165	210	260
12 Thigh clearance	125	150	175	115	145	170
13 Top of knees, height above floor	480	525	575	455	500	540
14 Popliteal height	385	425	470	355	395	440
15 Front of knees	210	280	350	325	295	365
16 Buttock - popliteal length	430	485	535	430	480	525
17 Rear of buttocks to front of knees	530	580	625	520	565	615
18 Seat width	305	350	395	310	370	430
Sitting and Standing						
19 Forward grip reach	700	755	805	640	685	735
20 Fingertip span	1605	1735	1860	1460	1570	1685
21 Shoulder width	400	445	485	345	385	380

Table 2.3
Dimensions of British Adults - Metric Handbook, Planning and Design Data.

Pointer B where the squiggle in rows 3, 4 and 5 indicates building users who could when new buildings are designed be conveniently accommodated.

The people in row 6 are independent wheelchair users.

In pointer C, with the squiggle denoting the people in rows 5, 4 and 3 whose needs may not be entirely taken care of when they use public buildings.

In row 7 are wheelchair users who need another person to help them, and those disabled people who drive electric scooters.

In row 8, having regard in particular to the usage of public toilets, are wheelchair users who need two people to help them.

The pointer D, indicating buildings that are entirely convenient for all their users.

Future of Ergonomic data

Although designers will always face design challenges on a project by project basis, the available anthropometric data to be used, to test ideas in terms of human factors, were strongly one-dimensional and two-dimensional based, which ultimately gave the average dimensions of male and female soldiers required for specifc tasks and jobs. Often studies were measurements based on soldiers dimensions. Showing averages and standard deviations of overhead reach distances to define cupboard height in furniture design. However, for a specific individuals care requirements this data will be limited.

New tools and techniques allow designers to make better use of anthropometric data by including a three dimensional representation of the human body (3D anthropometry) and take into account how the body moves though space over time. A focus on how specific detailed anthropometric research can be used as a tool during the design process can be initiated by the demands for certain data and requirements during the design process.

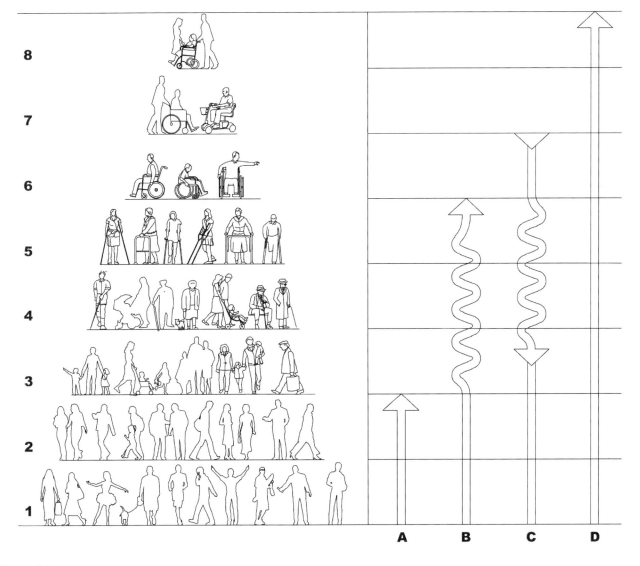

Figure 2.9
The bottom-up route to universal design - Universal Design

3. Access

Introduction

The main focus of this guide and the wider Assisted Living Innovation Platform (ALIP) project is centred on the developments in existing and emerging technologies allowing people to remain in their home environments for longer.

Whilst the overarching principles of this research programme is supportive emerging technologies, ultimately there is a requirement to address the issue of physical 'access' within the residential and built environments in which these products are set to work, the following section provides information and guidance on accessible residential buildings and their surrounding environments.

Accessible & Adaptable Design

Accessible and Adaptable are terms used to refer to housing or features in housing intended for use by people who are less able through illness, age or disability. Each term has different meanings and purposes. The differences are subtle but important. They are frequently used, interchangeable and sometimes misunderstood.

Accessible Design

Accessible generally means that the dwelling meets prescribed requirements for accessible housing. Mandatory requirements for accessible housing can vary and are found at national, local and general guidance levels for residential building models.

Accessible features in dwellings include items such as wide doors, sufficient clear floor space for wheelchairs, lower worktops, seating for bathing, grab bars in bathrooms, knee space under kitchen sinks, audible and visual signals, switches and controls in easily reached locations, level entrances and accessible routes through the house. Most accessible features are permanently fixed in place and apparent in the home.

Adaptable Design

Some accessible features such as knee spaces under sinks and counters and grab bars in bathrooms are obvious and change the appearance of accessible dwellings and how they are used. Dwelling units required to be accessible are intended to be usable by anyone and not held open exclusively for people with specific needs and requirements.

An adaptable dwelling unit has the potential for all the accessible features that a fixed accessible dwelling has but allows some items to be omitted or concealed until needed, so the dwellings can be better matched to individuals needs when required.

In an adaptable dwelling, wide doors, level access, controls and switch locations and other access features must be built in. Grab bars however, can be omitted and installed when needed. Because the necessary construction has already been provided, the bars can simply be screwed in place without opening existing walls to install reinforcing.

Adaptable design means readily adjusted. It does not allow building inaccessible dwellings on the promise that they will be removed or remodelled for accessibility upon request. Adaptable features are those that can be adjusted in a short time without involving structural or finished material changes.

A Home for Life

Building for Life is a tool for assessing the design quality of homes and neighbourhoods in England. It was developed by the Commission for Architecture and the Built Environment (CABE), with partners the Home Builders Federation, the Civic Trust and Design for Homes.

The Building for Life tool comprises 20 areas of criteria to assess the design quality of new housing developments. The approach embodied by the criteria is based on urban design principles and quality issues set out on national Planning Policies. The criteria also relate to other standards for housing design, including the BREEAM EcoHomes standard, the Code for Sustainable Homes, Lifetime Homes and Secured by Design.

"Manual for Streets (2007): "Street layouts…should aim to make the environment self explanatory to all users. Features such as public art, planting and architectural style can assist navigation while possibly reducing the need for signs." p116.

A design for a new residential development should incorporate a simple and clear identity and be easy for the residents and visitors to understand a route within the site.

Wayfinding within the residential setting can be enhanced through the use of simple key indicators or tools such as Focal points, clear views and routes, lighting, colour and scents.

Complicated winding site layouts can encourage vehicle movement and discourage walking. The monotonous use of similar housing types can create confusion when navigating around a site.

Adaptability

For houses the fundamental issue is adaptability and conversion. Can existing and new build homes incorporate the future inclusion of level entrances, a ground floor WC or bathroom, wider doors, the installation of a stair lift or through floor lift? As technology becomes an integral part of our daily lives, can the construction material of the home incorporate common technologies such as 'WiFi', without creating 'not spots' around the home?

Car Parking

Designated parking bays should be indicated via the use of contrasting markings in colour and luminance against the background. Parking bays designated to a particular property should be located as close as possible to the pedestrian routes or close to the dwelling entrance. Dropped kerbs are to be incorporated to assist disabled people transferring from vehicle to wheelchair and onto the pavement.

A safe drop off point should be considered close to the main accessible entrance.

Payment systems for car parks should be accessible for disabled use.

On-Street Parking

On street parking bays must be 4200mm x 3600mm when parallel to the kerb.

Designated disable parking bays should be clearly marked 'DISABLED' in addition to a sign with a Blue Badge disabled symbol. Traffic Sign regulations 2002 provide further information.

Off-Street Parking

Disabled parking bays within covered car parks must be located to pedestrian routes.

Disabled parking bays within new developments should adhere to the following ratio.

1-10 bays, inc. 1 accessible bay.
11-25 bays, inc. 2 accessible bay.
26-50 bays, inc. 4 accessible bay.
51-75 bays, inc. 8 accessible bay.
76-100 bays, inc. 12 accessible bay.
100+ bays, inc. 12% accessible bay.

Internal Surfaces and Finishes

Hard surfaces can cause sound reverberations and increased background noise levels, which can cause difficulties for people with hearing impairments. A mixture of hard and soft surfaces should be considered.

Deep pile or excessively grooved carpets should be avoided as they will cause traction difficulties for wheelchair users. Carpets should be of shallow dense pile. All floor coverings should be firmly fixed.

Junctions between different flooring materials should be considered when detailing to avoid a trip hazard or obstacle for people with mobility or visual impairments. Where a mat-well is proposed, the mat should be of a limited non-compressible material with the finish level equal to the surrounding floor finish.

The proposed design for finished materials to the floors, walls and furniture should avoid incorporating distinctive patterns and shapes which could disorientate residents.

The layout of high density residential buildings should consider a wayfinding map incorporating textures and distinctive colours for residents and visitors with sight impairments.

Contrasts in surface colours, material and luminance should be considered. This approach should be adopted for switches, sockets and controls.

Communication Systems

Alarm systems should incorporate a visual alarm in addition to the audible alarm when installed in public areas. A visual alarm should be incorporated into alarm systems within lifts and toilets and all areas requiring emergency communication. All communication and emergency systems must be installed by trained and certified staff.

Wayfinding

Buildings designed with a logical layout can directly assist wayfinding, particularly for people with sight impairments and people with learning difficulties. Additional information can be conveyed through colour, communication systems, maps, models, and guides.

Colour can be used to signal where certain features can be found within a building. For example, all walls within core areas containing stairs, lifts and WC's could be painted a particular colour to help orientation.

Visual information can be provided by distinguishing floor, wall, and ceiling planes and decorative features.

Tactile maps and models of the interior layout of buildings, particularly those of architectural interest - aid the comprehension of the building for those with sight impairment.

Lighting

Good lighting is essential for everyone for visibility and safety. Lighting systems can be used to accentuate interior colour, tone and texture.

Entrance areas, foyers and lobbies should be used as transition areas to enable people to adjust to changes in lighting levels from inside to outside, and outside to inside, and to lighting levels within different parts of a building. In public buildings, electronic monitoring of lighting levels inside and outside should be considered.

Use light colours for walls and ceilings as these help to reflect and diffuse the light. Gloss finishes should not be used on walls or ceilings.

Lights should be positioned where they do not cause glare, reflection, shadows or pools of light and dark.

Uplighters should not be used at street or floor level but should be positioned above 2000mm from ground floor level.

Fluorescent light fittings should be screened, maintained to avoid flicker, and located to avoid interference with hearing enhancement systems.

All lighting systems should be compatible with hearing enhancement and radio frequency systems.

Where possible the lamps should have a good colour rendering properties, for example, use 'daylight' lamps.

Lighting the entrance to a dwelling

The entrance to a dwelling, whether on an individual plot or within a block of flats, should be lit artificially.

A good location for a luminaire is to the side or above a doorway where the door is flush to the doorway.

A well lit entrance permits callers to be identified and assists both residents and visitors.

Lighting of communal entrances to a block of flats

Artificial lighting must be provided to the communal entrance to a block of flats enabling residents to identify callers. The lighting system should be connected to a PIR light sensor with sufficient overrun time giving automatic illumination from dusk to dawn. Light levels should achieve a 200 lux to the face of the caller and to the entrance lock mechanism and key hole.

Acoustics

Consideration of the acoustic properties of buildings, as well as the specification of hearing enhancements systems, can benefit people with hearing impairments.

In order to allow people with hearing impairments to maximise their residual hearing, it is important to keep background noise to a minimum.

Sounds can be useful for people with visual impairments. For example, the sound of a lift arrival bell locates the lift, the sound of footstep informs that a person is approaching.

Additional technical information must be sought from induction loop manufacturers. Some systems may allow sounds to be picked up by hearing aid users in adjacent rooms.

Pavements and Access Routes

Pedestrian routes should have an even spread of lighting and remain barrier free and where possible should be distinguishable zones between pavement and vehicle routes. When considering the location of lighting care should be given to glare and avoidance of large areas of cast shadow. Free standing lighting columns and bollards should be visually contrasting against their background.

Access routes should have firm, slip-resistant and reasonably smooth surface, with the exception of tactile paving. Cobbles, bare earth, sand and unbounded gravel should not be used as finished surfaces. Consideration must be given for the potential settlement of below ground materials when incorporating abutment surfaces and joints.

Joints between paving surfaces and adjoining materials should be level between finishes. Any access route with a gradient steeper than 1 in 20 should conform with the recommendations set out in Approved Document Part M, ramped access. Gradients falling access routes from building across a footpath should not exceed 1 in 50 (2%), the exception occurs in a dropped kerb situation. Consideration must be given to colour differentiation between the footpath and the kerb edge and up stands greater than 100mm.

The width of access routes may vary depending on circumstances, new developments and existing developments with a statement on pavement width within the supporting Design & Access statement.

The minimum width for main access routes in new developments should be 1800mm. Allowing wheelchair users and pedestrians to pass, although 2000mm is the preferred width.

The width of the pavement can be reduced further to 1500mm with the allowance for passing points every 25 metres.

The choice of planting is to be selected to assist wayfinding and positioned in proximity to street furniture or building entrances as natural forms of signposting around developments. Colour, aroma, distinctive forms and even texture of planting will all assist as directional landmarks, however provision must be taken

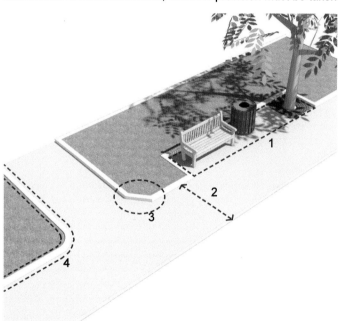

Figure 3.1
Pathways and Access routes

to ensure an adequate maintenance programme is adopted to prevent planting from overhanging footpaths.

When considering the placement of street furniture within a development, the location should be situated to provide visual landmarks. Furniture needs to be set back from the footpath without causing potential hazards.

Entrance and exiting doors and windows must not swing out into an access route. Should an access route pass below the underside of a projecting wall, building canopy, tree or sign then a minimum clearance of 2500mm must be allowed for.

1 – Obstacles recessed from access routes
2 – 1800mm / 2000mm wide pavements. (1500mm if passing places for prams/wheelchairs are provided.)
3 – Defined path edge with an up stand 50mm – 100mm high.
4 – Splayed or rounded angles to adjoining routes.

Entering a dwelling or a multi-storey block of flats

Weather Protection
The main entrance to a house or the communal entrance to a block of flats should contain some form of weather protection, a canopy or recess allowing momentary shelter for people prior to entering the building. Canopy support posts or structures should not provide obstacles to circulation routes towards the entrance door.

The external entrance to a house or block of flats must contain a level entrance area within the entrance recess or below an entrance canopy. The level landing area ensures that a wheelchair or pram remains stable when the user accesses the entrance.

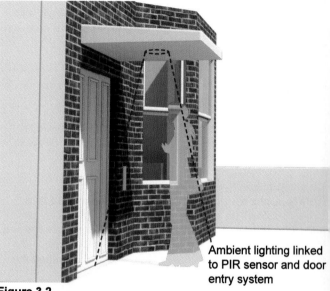

Ambient lighting linked to PIR sensor and door entry system

Figure 3.2
Dwelling entrance canopy

An accessible level threshold must be provided at the building entrance. A maximum 15mm threshold up stand maybe incorporated where a level threshold cannot be achieved.

The provision of entrance matting to remove water and debris from shoes and wheelchairs must finish level with the adjacent floor finish. If the matting is surface laid, has chamfered edges that do not provide trip hazards.

The responsibility of the successful design and construction for accessible entrance thresholds lies with the Builder / Architect in accordance with the recommendations set out in the Approved Document Part M.

External landing
A level external landing must be at the entrance of a block of flats or an individual house to ensure that a wheelchair remains stable when the user is reaching the door bell, unlocking the door or using access control/call systems. A canopy must cover the width of the landing.

For a block of flats, the external landing should be at least 1500 mm × 1500 mm clear of any door swings to enable a wheelchair user to turn.

Note:
Guidance on the selection, planning, installation and maintenance of entrance flooring systems is given in BS 7953. All entrances should be illuminated and have accessible level access over the threshold level, the main entrance should be covered.

Access control and call systems

Access control systems

Where door entry systems are installed, they should, where practicable, be located on the latch edge of the door, either on the door face or on the adjacent wall. The activation pad should be positioned within 200 mm of the door frame (or aperture where there is a glazed façade), at a height of between 900 mm and 1050 mm from the finished floor level.

Alarms

It is important that people with visual or hearing impairments can be alerted in case of an emergency.

Use of emergency alarms must be backed up by a suitable evacuation strategy for all occupants, taking into account all disabilities.

Door entry systems

The positioning of the entry system should be, where possible, located on the latch side of the entrance door or adjacent wall. The door opening activation button should be located within 200mm of the latch side of the door at a height from finished floor level of 900mm – 1050mm.

It is important that people with visual and/or hearing impairments can be alerted in case of emergency.

Use of emergency alarms must be backed up by a suitable evacuation strategy for all occupants.

The entry phone system should contrast with the background setting.

NOTE:
Video entry phone systems provide additional benefits for the person answering the call, as well as for the person wishing to gain entry.

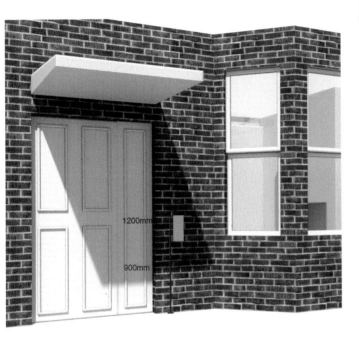

Figure 3.3
Dwelling entrance access control system

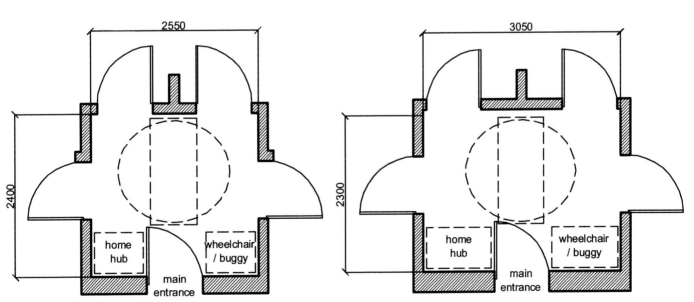

Figures 3.4 & 3.5
HUBUGHALL - refer to chapter 8 'Lifehome 21'

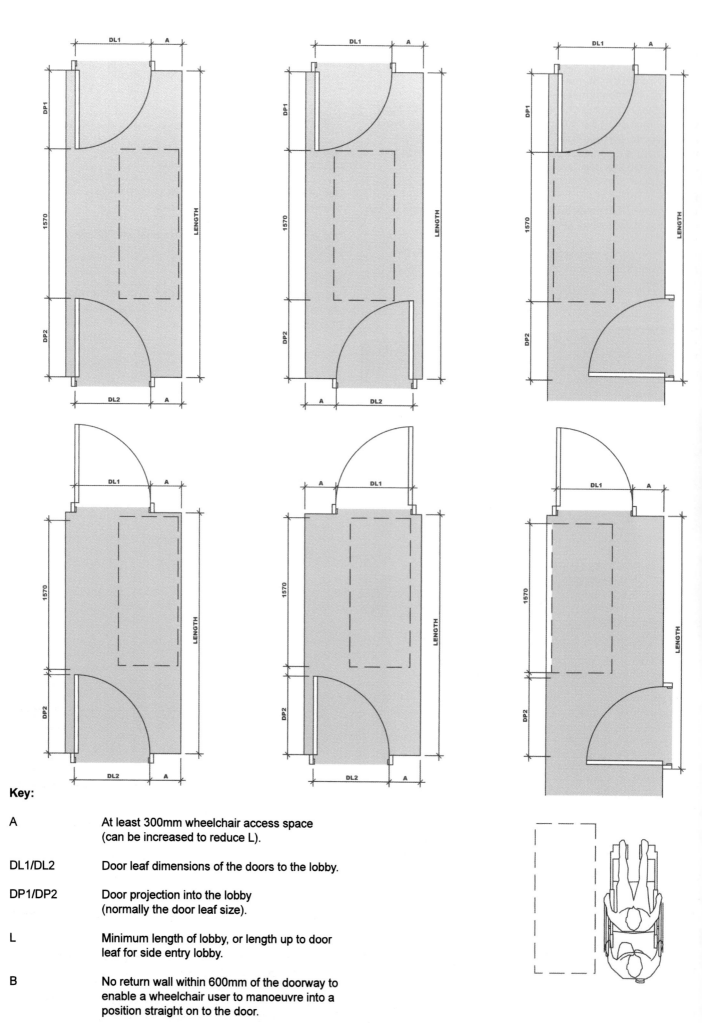

Key:

A   At least 300mm wheelchair access space
(can be increased to reduce L).

DL1/DL2   Door leaf dimensions of the doors to the lobby.

DP1/DP2   Door projection into the lobby
(normally the door leaf size).

L   Minimum length of lobby, or length up to door
leaf for side entry lobby.

B   No return wall within 600mm of the doorway to
enable a wheelchair user to manoeuvre into a
position straight on to the door.

Note: The 1570mm dimension represents the length of an
occupied wheelchair with a companion or assistant.

Figure 3.6
Key dimensions for lobbies with single leaf doors -
The building regulations - Part M

DESIGN FOR ACCESS 2 – Dwellings

Design for Access 2

The following section outlines the approach undertaken by Manchester City Council in addressing the Access issues when dealing with residential developments. The Design and Access 2 document sets out aspirational standards which will help to promote accessible design. It is also intended that these standards will be pro-active in the national debate concerning the statutory framework needed to secure access for all. The guidance document was first published in 2000 with a revised edition in 2004 reflecting government guidance such as BS 8300:2001 and Part M of the Building Regulations. The document is designed to used by parties implementing access strategies within Manchester City Council portfolio of buildings, be they commercial, leisure facilities or residential environments.

To increase the amount of housing stock in Manchester which meets the requirements of disabled people the Council has adopted policies which promote the provision of housing which is accessible for all visitors and which is also capable of adaptation to become a home for life.

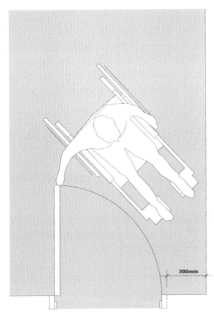

Figure 3.7
Effective door width requirements of doors -
The building regulations, Part M

To comply with these policies the following requirements apply:

All new housing developments on land which the City Council owns, including disposal sites, or in projects in which the City Council has an interest, must be accessible for all visitors.

All new housing developments on land which the City Council owns, including disposal sites, or in projects in which the City Council has an interest, must be capable of adaptation for occupation by disabled people.

All refurbishments and conversions of properties which the City Council owns, or in which the City Council has an interest, which include residential use, should seek to meet the standards in this section, or must demonstrate by means of an Access Statement why they cannot be met.

Provision for adaptation to meet the requirements of disabled people, a dwelling should have sufficient space to offer a choice of accessible layouts. To widen the choice of accessible housing, a number of options could be considered for bedroom, toilet,

shower and bathroom provisions.
If the future occupier is known they should be consulted on the layout and fitting-out of kitchens, bedrooms and bathrooms, and about any other personal requirements.

If the future occupier is not known all the following requirements should be met in all new dwellings to ensure that they are capable of adaptation.

A suitable, safe location should be identified within each dwelling for parking and charging a power wheelchair or scooter.

The design of all new dwellings that are on more than one level should incorporate provision for a future stair lift, and also a suitably identified space of minimum 1400mm x 1100mm for the future installation of a house lift (through-the-floor lift) from the ground to the first floor. The proposed provision must satisfy all normal Building Regulations requirements.

At least one accessible bedroom should be provided in each dwelling, of minimum dimensions 4000mm x 4000mm.

Where a development incorporates dwellings with three or more bedrooms, a proportion of these should have a second bedroom of minimum dimensions 3000mm x 3000mm.

Where possible, ensuite facilities should be provided, of minimum dimensions 2000mm x 2000mm, and should include a WC, a wash hand basin and a shower.

Where only one bathroom is provided it should have minimum dimensions of 2700mm x 2500mm to allow for the provision of a WC, a wash hand basin, a bath and a shower.

Walls in bathrooms, showers and toilets should be constructed to take adaptations such as grab rails.

Ceilings, walls and floors in bedrooms, toilets, showers and bathrooms should be constructed to take adaptations such as track hoists.

Circulation space of minimum 1800mm x 1800mm should be available in kitchens after fitting-out.

On each floor there should be no stepped changes of level.

Internal doors should have a minimum clear opening of 800mm. The effective clear opening should be clear of projections. Double doors may be fitted, if preferred.

Window sills should be no more than 900mm above floor level. Any glazing less than 900mm above floor level should be safety glass.

The width of internal stairs should be minimum 900mm.

Do not use open risers or open recesses under stairs.

A step should not overlap the one below.

There should be a continuous handrail on both sides of the stairs and on landings.

For new-build or complete refurbishment, the use of residential sprinklers should be considered.

Switches, sockets and service controls for heating, lighting, radio, television, telephones and computers etc, should be centered at 900mm above floor level.

For newbuild or complete refurbishment, the use of residential

sprinklers should be considered.
Lifts – Passenger & Platform lifts

These standards are for passenger lifts, platform lifts and goods lifts.

Passenger lifts provide access between levels and storey's. A disabled person needs sufficient space and time to enter and leave a passenger lift, particularly when sharing it with other people. Lift sizes should therefore be chosen to suit the anticipated density of use of the building and the requirements of disabled people.

Platform lifts (lifting platforms) should be used only where space is restricted and access is only between two levels.

Stair lifts, which follow the line of a stair, should not be used in buildings other than dwellings. Where they are used in dwellings, they should be designed to meet the individual's requirements. Internal stairs should also be provided as an alternative means of access to other levels, designed to Part M standards.

Passenger Lifts
Internal dimensions should be minimum 2000mm wide x 1400mm deep x 2000mm high with maximum 15mm finishes.

For specific constrained circumstances, for example, in refurbishment schemes, minimum internal dimensions of 1100mm wide x 1400mm deep x 2000mm high would be sufficient.

There must be an unobstructed area in front of the lift entrance of 1800mm x 1800mm.

The area in front of and to the side of the lift must be kept clear of obstructions to allow access to the controls.

Seating should be provided outside and near to the lift.

Illuminated and audible systems to identify floor levels should be positioned inside and outside the lift.

Internal handrails must be provided 900mm above floor level.

Where a lift has a single door, a mirror, with minimum dimensions of 1000mm wide x 1000mm high, should be positioned inside the lift on the wall opposite the door at no higher than 900mm above floor level.

Doors should include a presence sensor and, where possible, have a minimum door opening time of 20 seconds. The door to the lift must provide a clear opening width of minimum 900mm. Except where space is constrained in refurbishment schemes lifts should use single or opposite doors only.

Call buttons outside the lift should preferably be on the right side of the door, should be colour and luminance contrasted with the surround, should have embossed symbols, and should be positioned no higher than 900mm.

Control buttons within the lift should be horizontal, centred at a height of 900mm above floor level, centrally placed on the lift walls, and preferably on both sides of the compartment. There should also be a standard vertical control panel near to the door.

All controls must be identifiable with raised and Braille symbols. The depth of embossing should be at least 1.5mm. The controls should be in a contrasting colour and luminance on non-reflective panels.

Figure 3.8
Through Floor knock out panel for future accommodation of lift/ flupper.

Lifts must have emergency communication systems, located no higher than 900mm above floor level, which provide audible and visual signals, explain how to make emergency calls and indicate, audibly and visually, when an emergency call has been received.

Flooring, wall and ceiling finishes should be opaque, non-reflective and slip resistant.

Lighting within lifts should avoid glare, reflection, shadows or pools of light.

At least one lift in each area of the building should be designed as an evacuation lift, with an independent power supply, and should be clearly indicated for this use.

Signage indicating the floor level should be provided on the wall opposite the lift doors on each landing.

Platform Lifts
An identified knock-out zone for a potential 'through the floor' lift from the entrance level to first floor, for example to a bedroom next to a bathroom.

Through-the-floor lifts are made to a range of different specifications. Lift retailers can be contacted for the most up to date specifications and dimensions.

Internal dimensions should be minimum of 1100mm wide x 1400mm deep.

There should be an unobstructed area in front of the lift entrance of 1800mm x 1800mm.

The area in front of and to the side of the lift should be kept clear of obstructions to allow access to the controls.

The door to the lift must provide a clear opening width of minimum 900mm.

The floor to the lift car must be level with the unobstructed area in front of the lift.

The lift car must be enclosed.

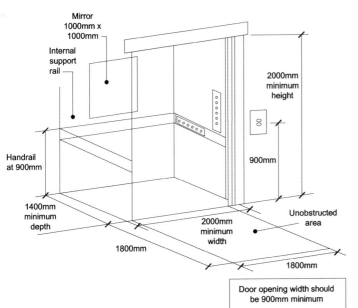

Mirror 1000mm x 1000mm

Internal support rail

2000mm minimum height

Handrail at 900mm

900mm

1400mm minimum depth

1800mm

2000mm minimum width

Unobstructed area

1800mm

Door opening width should be 900mm minimum

Figure 3.9
Passenger Lifts - Manchester City Council, Design for Access 2

Flooring, wall and ceiling finishes should be opaque, non-reflective and slip-resistant.

The controls must be capable of use independently by the user and set no higher than 900mm above floor level.

The doors must not require the simultaneous operation of two mechanisms to open them.

The door opening and closing system should be automatic.

The lift must incorporate audible and visual alarm and emergency systems.

There must be clear instructions for use, with a font of at least 14 point sans-serif, and an audible and visual alarm system.

Where vision panels are fitted the base of the vision panel should be no higher than 500mm above floor level, and should extend to a minimum height of 1500mm.

New Technological Developments
Flupper is a human powered system for moving between floors yet, it requires less than 10% of the effort compared to stairs. Proven in a study with the Biodynamics Department of Imperial College / Charing Cross Hospital. Flupper: 3.6m in < 8sec - stairs: 3.6m in > 17sec.

This means that many of those unable to take stairs can use flupper.

Figure 3.10
Flupper - Rombout Frieling, Royal College of Art.
Current research being developed by the RCA and others

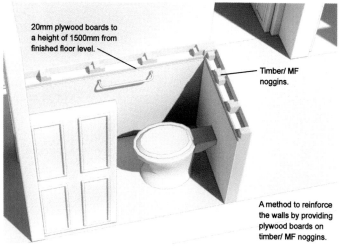

20mm plywood boards to a height of 1500mm from finished floor level.

Timber/ MF noggins.

A method to reinforce the walls by providing plywood boards on timber/ MF noggins.

Note: Walls in bathrooms and ground floor WC's must be capable of supporting adaptions and additions such as handrails.

Figure 3.11
Partition wall construction to ground floor WC

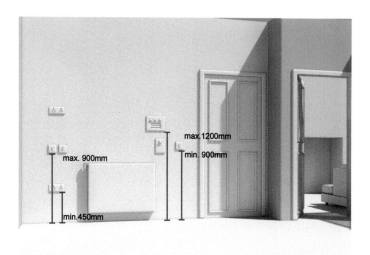

max.1200mm

max. 900mm

min. 900mm

min.450mm

Figure 3.12
Heights of Switches and Sockets in accordance with Part M of the Building Regulations

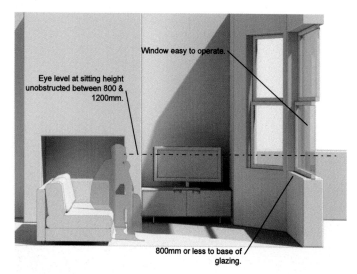

Window easy to operate.

Eye level at sitting height unobstructed between 800 & 1200mm.

800mm or less to base of glazing.

Figure 3.13
Height of window transoms allowing a view from a wheelchair or chair - BS8300

4. Space Standards

Housing Standards

Introduction
In recent years, it has become apparent and widely recognised that residential design needs to address a broad range of people and various abilities. Future housing should be able to adapt to the differing needs and requirements of the users, no matter of their age, strength or agility. This design approach strives to make the day-to-day home living and home tasks possible and safer for everyone.

These goals are no less significant for affordable housing and, in fact, may even be more critical for households that lack the financial and social resources to effectively deal with dramatic life changes from sickness and injury, effects of ageing, or support other family members. The ability to remain physically independent is a critical part of being financially independent.

The continuing problem of the provision of decent affordable housing for low income households is compounded by the availability of few homes that respond to the diverse needs of individuals with disabilities. For these people, finding housing that also supports their activities can be difficult.

Residents living in homes with a disabled family member can find themselves facing expensive modifications such as ramps, wider doorways and usable bathrooms. New housing that supports residents now and which doesn't require future modifications are clearly superior to current models of residential design. For housing to address these needs all home design should recognise and accept that being human means that there is no one model individual whose characteristics remain static through their lifetime.

Whereas the Manchester City Council 'Design for Access 2' guide looks to address the issues of access in and around the city dealing with both residential and commercial access, the London Housing Design guide is clearly focused on providing specific guidance on new housing standards for public housing, procured by public bodies. The London Housing design guide is not a statement of Planning Policy but will be aligned with the new London Plan and Housing Supplementary Planning Guidance and the HCA design standards review. The LHD guide has integrated a wide range of housing standards into one document. This guide looks to amalgamate Lifetime Homes, Housing Quality Indicators, Building for Life and the Code for Sustainable Homes into one document and provides focused direction for new space standards and the increasing challenge of sustainability within the residential sector.

London Housing Design Guide
It is not just about providing space, but ensuring that space can be flexibly used to respond to varying needs and that development takes an inclusive approach for all users.

Housing in a diverse city: A mix of housing sizes, types and tenures at a range of densities are needed to respond to Londoners' diverse needs.

Dwelling space: New minimum internal space standards are set out, along with further requirements and guidance on the size and layout of different rooms to ensure greater flexibility of space in the home.

Appropriate Density

Requirements
Development proposals must demonstrate how densities of residential accommodation reflect a sound understanding of public transport accessibility level (PTAL), accessibility to local amenities and services, and appropriateness to physical context.

Residential Mix
Developments should also cater for various needs by having a mix of housing tenure including affordable housing and specialist housing such as the provision of wheelchair accessible dwellings.

Mix of Uses
Neighbourhoods are successful where people are able to fulfil daily tasks within a comfortable walking distance such as getting to a bus stop or station, food shopping, and relaxing in a park, café or pub.

Proposals for larger residential developments should assess the need for community and ancillary services such as local health and education facilities, and their distance from a development to determine what could be integrated into a development.

Entrance and Approach
Paths from the street and car parking should have a suitable width and gradient for wheelchair users, with a level landing in front of any entrance door.

Requirements
Any external footpaths to a communal entrance within the curtilage of a development should be a minimum of 1200mm wide.

The approach to all entrances should be level or gently sloping with a level landing of 1500mm x 1500mm clear of any door swing.
Lifetime Homes Criteria 2 and 4, www.lifetimehomes.org.uk

Shared Circulation

Design of Shared Circulation
Common entrances should lead to a hall large enough for people to manoeuvre with shopping and baby buggies, and for wheelchair users to move with ease.

Access controls
Access control systems should be accessible to disabled people in terms of height and use of tactile numbers.

Management and Maintenance

Requirements
Communal circulation corridors should be a minimum of 1200mm wide.

Lift provision
A minimum of two lifts per core will be expected where dwellings are entered at or above the eighth floor (ninth storey) in order to reduce waiting times and to ensure accessibility for wheelchair users, older people and families with small children is maintained if one lift is out of service.

Requirements
For all buildings with dwellings entered at the first and second floor (second and third storey), space should be identified within or adjacent to the common circulation for the future installation of a wheelchair accessible lift.

Where lifts are provided, at least one lift in each access core must be wheelchair accessible with internal dimensions of 1100mm x 1400mm and clear landing entrance of 1500 x 1500mm.
Lifetime Homes, www.lifetimehomes.org.uk, Criterion 2.

DD266, Design for Accessible Housing: Lifetime Homes Code of Practice, British Standards Institution, 2007.
Lifetime Homes, www.lifetimehomes.org.uk, Criterion 5.

Car Parking

Blue badge parking bays should be located adjacent to lift cores to keep travel distances to a minimum.

Cycle Storage

Requirements

All developments should aim to provide storage for cycles as follows;

1 per flat.
1 per 1-2 bedroom house.
2 per 3+ bedroom house.

Cycle parking should be secure, sheltered and adequately lit with convenient access to the street.

Internal Floor Area

The space requirements aim to ensure rooms are large enough to take on varying uses.

The space standards in this guide are minimum requirements.

Requirements

The following space standards must be met as a minimum in new developments. For dwellings designed for more than 6 people, allow approximately 10sq.m. per person.

Standard based upon spatial analysis of furniture requirements from Housing Quality Indicators Version 4, (former) Housing Corporation, April 2007 and Lifetime Homes criteria.

Minimum dwelling by floor area	Dwelling type (bedroom/persons)	Essential GIA (sq.m)
Flats	1b2p	50
	2b3p	61
	2b4p	70
	3b4p	74
	3b5p	86
	3b6p	100
	4b5p	90
	4b6p	99
2 storey houses	2b4p	83
	3b4p	86
	3b5p	96
	4b5p	100
	4b6p	107
3 storey houses	3b5p	102
	4b5p	106
	4b6p	113

Table 4.1
Internal floor area - London Housing Design Guide

Layout and Adaptability

Flexibility is the potential to use the rooms of a home in a variety of ways; for example, the ability to rearrange furniture in a room, make space to put up guests, convert a double bedroom into twin bedroom, or create suitable spaces for work and study. Flexibility is determined by space and room layout, and also by the number of rooms in a home. Homes where the living areas and circulation spaces are entirely open-plan will not necessarily create the greatest degree of flexibility when the home is in use.

Designers should aim to provide built-in adaptability by designing the structure to allow new openings to be made in internal walls with relative ease. The roof space of houses with pitched roofs should be designed to allow conversion.

Requirements

Plans should demonstrate that dwellings will accommodate the furniture, access and activity space requirements.

Dwelling plans should demonstrate how the construction of the building will allow for the internal reorganisation of rooms of the extension of the dwelling.
Based on Building for Life criteria no. 18.

Circulation in the Home

Requirements

The width of the doorways and hallways should conform to the specifications below:

The clear opening width of the front door should be at least 800mm.

A 300mm nib is required beside the leading edge (latch side) of all doors at entrance level.

All internal doors should have a clear opening width of at least 775mm.

All hallways and corridors inside a dwelling should have a clear width of at least 1050mm.

The design of dwellings over more than one storey should provide space for provision of a stair lift, and a suitably identified space for a through-the-floor lift from the ground to the first floor.

Based on Lifetime Homes, www.lifetimehomes.org.uk Criterion 6.

Design of Accessible Housing: Lifetime HOME Code of Practice, British Standards Institute, December 2007 (the DD 266 requirements for door and corridor widths is clearer and more succinct than the current Lifetime Homes standard).

Design of Accessible Housing: Lifetime Home Code of Practice, British Standards Institute, December 2007.

Lifetime Homes, www.lifetimehomes.org.uk, Criterion 12.

Living / Dining / Kitchen

The minimum width of a room used as a living room is 3.2m at the narrowest point.

Maximum glazing cill height of 800mm from the floor.
There should be space for turning a wheelchair in dining areas and living rooms and adequate circulation space for wheelchairs elsewhere.

Floor area for the aggregate of the living/dining area are:	(sq.m)
1 person / 2 person	23
3 person	25
4 person	27
5 person	29
6 person	31

Table 4.2
Floor areas for living / kitchen / dining - London Housing Design Guide
Lifetime Homes, www.lifetimehomes.org.uk, Criterion 7, 8, 15

A living room or kitchen-dining room should be at entrance level.

Living room window glazing should begin at 800mm or lower and windows should be easy to open and operate.

Quality Standards: Delivering Quality Places, (former) English Partnerships, November 2007, Page 16.

Bedroom
The inimum floor areas – 8.4 sq.m. for a single bedroom and 12.8 sq.m. for a double and twin bedrooms.
Double and twin bedrooms have the same minimum floor area and both should have a minimum width of 3m.

Requirements
The minimum area of a single bedroom should be 8.4 sq.m. The minimum area of a double bedroom should be 12.8 sq.m.

The minimum width of a double and twin bedrooms should be 3 metres at the narrowest point.

In homes over more than one storey, there should be space on the entrance level that could be used as a convenient bed-space.

The design should provide a reasonable route for a potential hoist from a main bedroom to the bathroom.
Lifetime Homes, www.lifetimehomes.org.uk, Criterion 9
Lifetime Homes, www.lifetimehomes.org.uk, Criterion 13

Bathroom
All dwellings should provide wheelchair accessible entrance level WC, with drainage provision enabling a shower to be fitted in the future.

Requirements
WCs should have a clear space of 1100mm in front and 700mm to one side to allow for a wheelchair user to manoeuvre.

Bathrooms should be designed to incorporate ease of access to the bath, WC and wash basin.

Bathroom layouts should indicate an area 1000mm x 1000mm for a shower (which may overlap with a bath) to allow an accessible shower to be installed in the future.

Walls in bathrooms and WCs should be capable of taking adaptations such as handrails. Wall reinforcements should be located between 300 and 1500mm from the floor.

Lifetime Homes, www.lifetimehomes.org.uk, Criterion 10, 11, 14.

Study and Work

Requirements
Dwelling plans should demonstrate that all homes are provided with adequate space and services to be able to work from home.

Wheelchair User Dwellings
The London Plan and the draft London Housing Strategy require all homes to be built to Lifetime Homes standards.

Disabled people, including wheelchair users, to visit the home and use the living room and bathroom.

Wheelchair users need more manoeuvring space, more storage space for additional equipment and larger rooms, which may make the footprint of a home designed to be wheelchair accessible different to other dwellings.

10% of new housing is designed to be wheelchair accessible or easily adaptable for a wheelchair user.

GLA's Best Practice Guide on Wheelchair Accessible Housing.

Space Standard Study - London Housing Guide

1 bed, 2 persons

Kitchen
Key to Items

AE Ancillary Equipment
BU Base Unit
DR Drawers
DW Dishwasher
FF Fridge Freezer
TC Tall Cupboard
TD Tumble Dryer
WM Washing Machine
CYL Hot Water Cylinder
SU Storage Unit

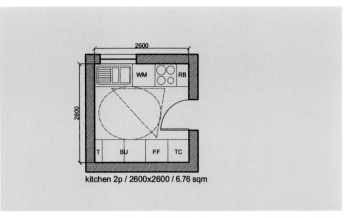

kitchen 2p / 2600x2600 / 6.76 sqm

Dining

Dining areas calculated as difference of kitchen-dining and kitchen.

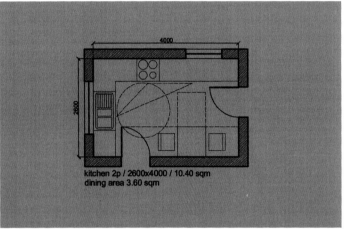

kitchen 2p / 2600x4000 / 10.40 sqm
dining area 3.60 sqm

Living

Combined kitchen/ living/ dining.

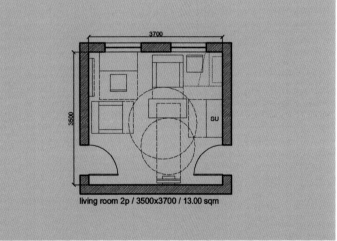

living room 2p / 3500x3700 / 13.00 sqm

Bathroom

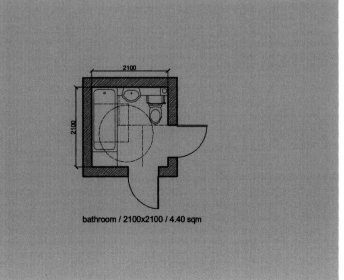

bathroom / 2100x2100 / 4.40 sqm

2 bed, 3 persons

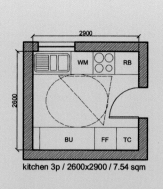

kitchen 3p / 2600x2900 / 7.54 sqm

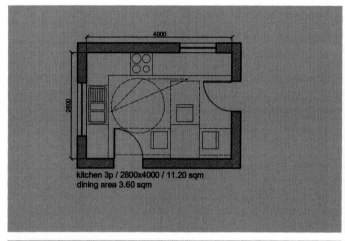

kitchen 3p / 2800x4000 / 11.20 sqm
dining area 3.60 sqm

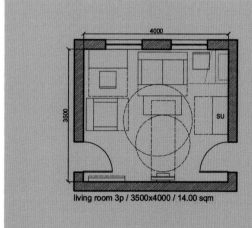

living room 3p / 3500x4000 / 14.00 sqm

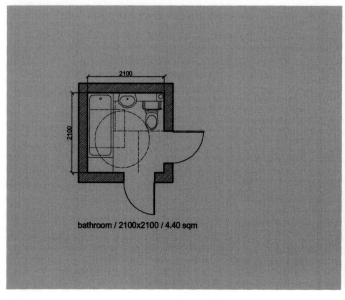

bathroom / 2100x2100 / 4.40 sqm

3 bed, 5 persons

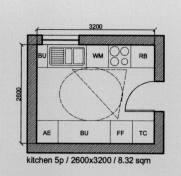

kitchen 5p / 2600x3200 / 8.32 sqm

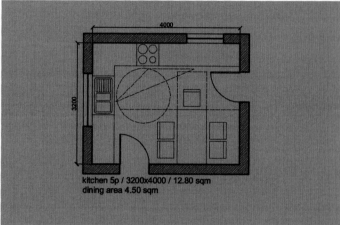

kitchen 5p / 3200x4000 / 12.80 sqm
dining area 4.50 sqm

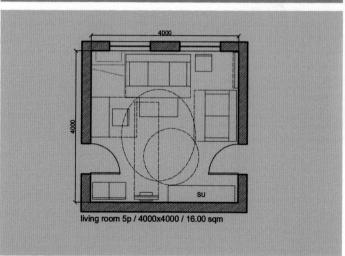

living room 5p / 4000x4000 / 16.00 sqm

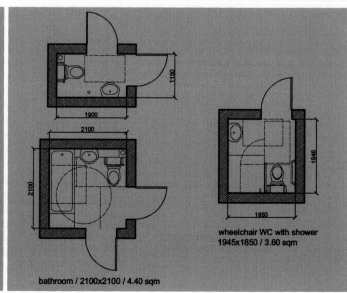

wheelchair WC with shower
1945x1850 / 3.60 sqm

bathroom / 2100x2100 / 4.40 sqm

Space Standard Study - London Housing Guide

4 bed, 6 persons

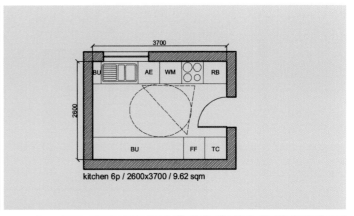

kitchen 6p / 2600x3700 / 9.62 sqm

Kitchen
Key to Items

AE Ancillary Equipment
BU Base Unit
DR Drawers
DW Dishwasher
FF Fridge Freezer
TC Tall Cupboard
TD Tumble Dryer
WM Washing Machine
CYL Hot Water Cylinder
SU Storage Unit

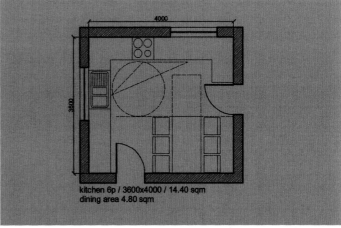

kitchen 6p / 3600x4000 / 14.40 sqm
dining area 4.80 sqm

Dining

Dining areas calculated as difference of kitchen-dining and kitchen.

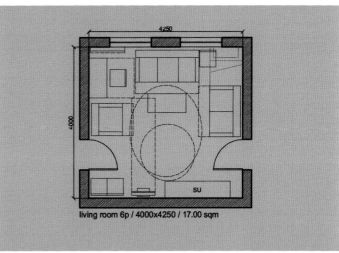

living room 6p / 4000x4250 / 17.00 sqm

Living

Combined kitchen/ living/ dining.

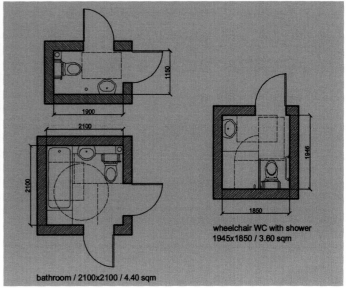

wheelchair WC with shower
1945x1850 / 3.60 sqm

bathroom / 2100x2100 / 4.40 sqm

Bathroom

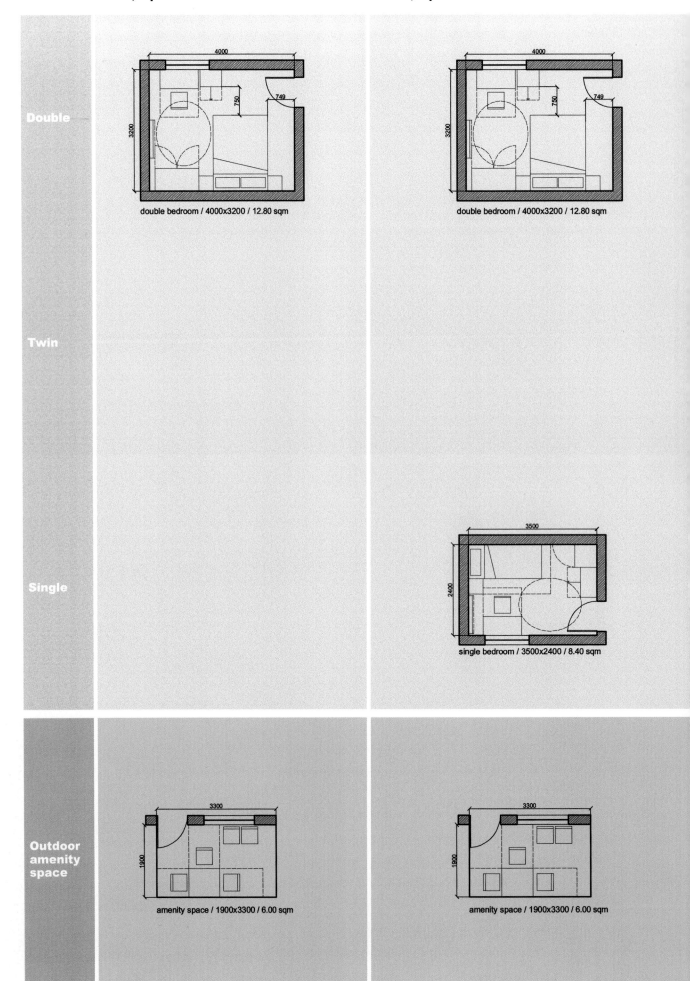

Double

4000

3200

750

749

double bedroom / 4000x3200 / 12.80 sqm

4000

3200

750

749

double bedroom / 4000x3200 / 12.80 sqm

Twin

Single

3500

2400

single bedroom / 3500x2400 / 8.40 sqm

Outdoor amenity space

3300

1900

amenity space / 1900x3300 / 6.00 sqm

3300

1900

amenity space / 1900x3300 / 6.00 sqm

3 bed, 5 persons   **4 bed, 6 persons**

Double

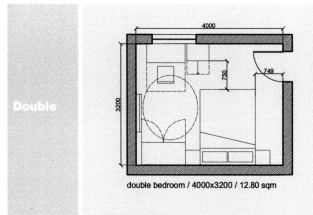

double bedroom / 4000x3200 / 12.80 sqm

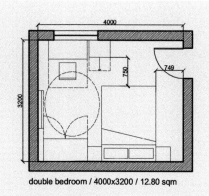

double bedroom / 4000x3200 / 12.80 sqm

Twin

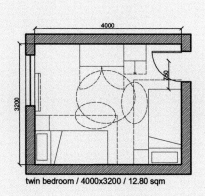

twin bedroom / 4000x3200 / 12.80 sqm

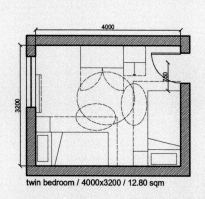

twin bedroom / 4000x3200 / 12.80 sqm

Single

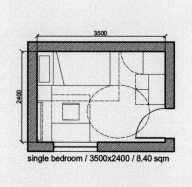

single bedroom / 3500x2400 / 8.40 sqm

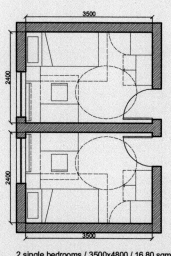

2 single bedrooms / 3500x4800 / 16.80 sqm

Outdoor amenity space

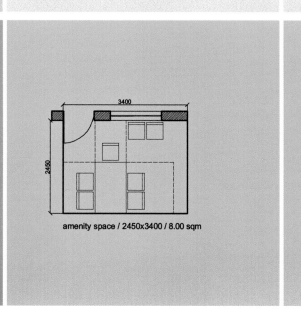

amenity space / 2450x3400 / 8.00 sqm

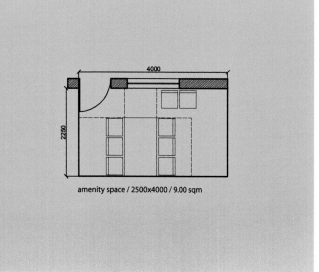

amenity space / 2500x4000 / 9.00 sqm

Circulation Layouts
(Stairs for 3m floor to floor height, 15 steps, 230 / 200mm)

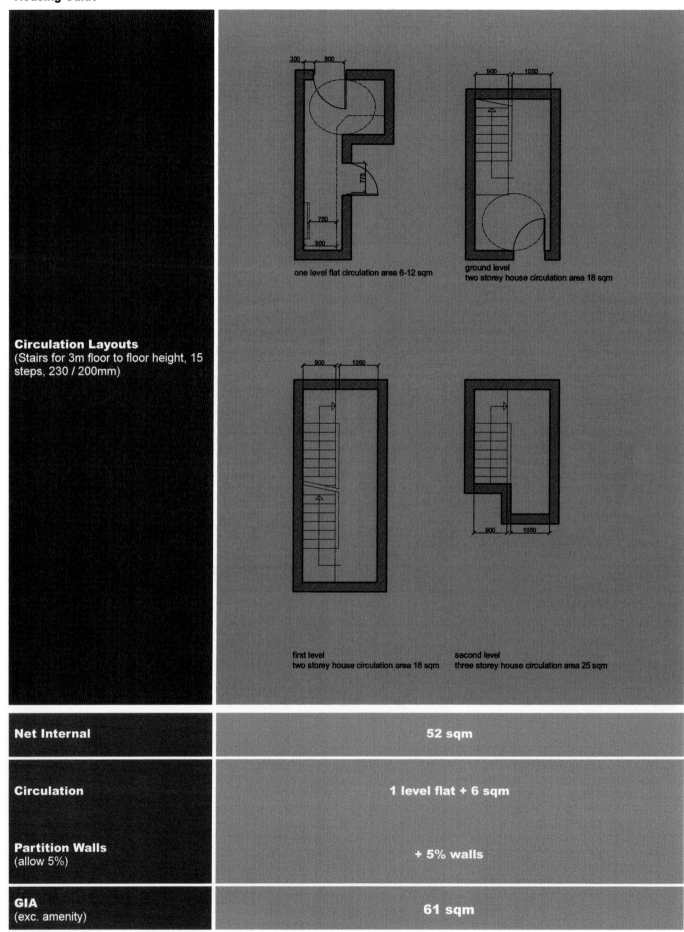

one level flat circulation area 6-12 sqm

ground level
two storey house circulation area 18 sqm

first level
two storey house circulation area 18 sqm

second level
three storey house circulation area 25 sqm

Net Internal	**52 sqm**
Circulation	**1 level flat + 6 sqm**
Partition Walls (allow 5%)	**+ 5% walls**
GIA (exc. amenity)	**61 sqm**

Space Standard Study - London Housing Guide

3 bed, 5 persons / 4 bed, 6 persons   HUBUGHALL

Circulation Layouts
(Stairs for 3m floor to floor height, 15 steps, 230 / 200mm)

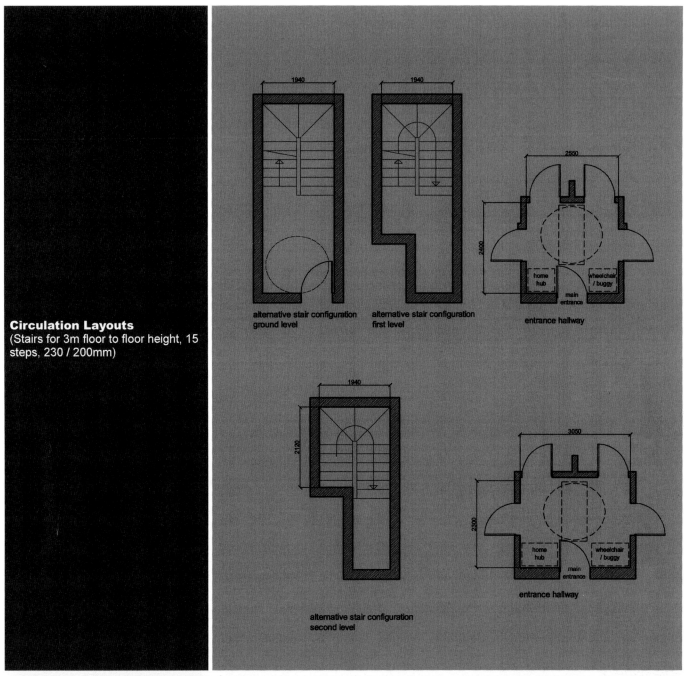

alternative stair configuration
ground level

alternative stair configuration
first level

entrance hallway

alternative stair configuration
second level

entrance hallway

Net Internal	71 sqm	71 sqm	72 sqm	82 sqm	83 sqm	83 sqm
Circulation	1 level flat + 11 sqm	2 storey house + 19 sqm	3 storey house + 25 sqm	1 level flat + 6 sqm	2 storey house + 19 sqm	3 storey house + 25 sqm
Partition Walls (allow 5%)	+ 5% walls	+ 5% walls	+ 5% walls	+ 5% walls	+ 5% walls	+ 5% walls
GIA (exc. amenity)	86 sqm	96 sqm	102 sqm	99 sqm	107 sqm	113 sqm

Note:
Additional 3 sqm required for the inclusion of HUBUGHALL
- refer to Lifehome 21 (page 90)

Table 4.3
Space Standard Study -
London Housing Design Guide / mae Architects

Type of Space	Furniture Schedule	Furniture Sizes (mm)	Dwelling Size						
			2p	3p	4p	5p	6p	7p	+
Living Space	arm chair - combination to equal one seat/person	850 x 850	2	1	1	2	1	2	+1
	settee - 2 seat (optional)	850 x 1300		1			1	1	
	settee - 3 seat (optional)	850 x 1850			1	1	1	1	
	TV - Approx. 26" flat	220 x 650	1	1	1	1	1	1	1
	coffee table	500 x 1050 or 750 diameter	1	1	1	1	1	1	1
	occasional table	450 x 450				1	1	1	1
	storage units	500 x 1000/ incrementally larger	1000	1000	1500	2000	2000	2000	+
	PC / laptop desk and chair	1050 x 500	1	1	1	1	1	1	1
	space for visitor's chair	450 x 450	2	2	2	2	2	2	2
Dining Space	dining chair	450 x 450	2	3	4	5	6	7	+
	dining table	800 x 800/ incrementally larger	800	1000	1200	1350	1500	1650	+
	sideboard (but not in dining kitchen)	450 x 1000/ incrementally larger	1000	1000	1200	1500	1500	1650	+
Bedrooms									
Double Bedroom	double bed	2000 x 1500	1	1	1	1	1	1	1
Optional	2 x single bed	2000 x 900							
	bedside table	400 x 400	2	2	2	2	2	2	2
	dressing table and chair / stool	500 x 1050	1	1	1	1	1	1	1
	chest of drawers	450 x 750	1	1	1	1	1	1	1
	double wardrobe - could be built in	600 x 1200	1	1	1	1	1	1	1
Optional	occasional cot space for family dwelling	600 x 1200			1	1	1	1	
Twin Bedroom	2 x single bed	2000 x 900			2	2	2	2	2
	bedside table	400 x 400			2	2	2	2	2
	chest of drawers	450 x 750			1	1	1	1	1
	table and chair / stool	500 x 1050			1	1	1	1	1
	double wardrobe - could be built in	600 x 1200			1	1	1	1	1
Single Bedroom	single bed	2000 x 900		1	1	1	1	1	1
	bedside table	400 x 400		1	1	1	1	1	1
	chest of drawers	450 x 750		1	1	1	1	1	1
	table and chair / stool	500 x 1050		1	1	1	1	1	1
	single wardrobe - could be built in	600 x 600		1	1	1	1	1	1
	Total bed spaces		2	3	4	5	6	7	+
Kitchen	(1) sink top drainer	600 x 1000	1000	1000	1000	1000	1000	1000	1000
	(2) cooker space	600 x 600	600	600	600	600	600	600	600
	(3) washing machine position / worktop	600 x 630	630	630	630	630	630	630	630
	(3a) tumble dryer / worktop	600 x 600			600	600	600	600	600
	(3a) dishwasher / worktop	600 x length	450	600	600	600	600	600	600
	(4) other base units	600 x length	1200	1600	1600	1600	2700	2700	+
	(5) ancillary equipment space	600 x length				600	1200	1200	1200
	(6) fridge / freezer space (space not in VOL)	600 x 600	600	600	600	600	600	600	600
	(7) broom cupboard (note this may be counted towards the tall storage requirement)	600 x 600 x 1950[H]	600	600	600	600	600	600	600
	(8) tray space	600 x 150	inc	inc	inc	inc	inc	inc	inc
	(9) recycling bins space	600 x length	300	300	300	600	600	600	600
	(10) length of fitments (items 1 to 9 [excl. 3a and 3b])		4930	5330	5330	6230	7330	7930	+
	(10a) length of fitments (items 1 to 9 [incl. 3a and 3b])		5380	6530	6530	7430	8530	9130	+
	(11) Volume - min capacity (cu.m.) (must include drawers) [excl. 3a and 3b]. Any wall units provided should be 300 deep and 450 above base units. Note: Item 3,5,6,7,9 may be in adjacent rooms to the kitchen		1.5	2	2.1	2.2	2.4	2.6	+
Bathroom	WC + cistern	500 x 700	1	1	1	1	1	1	1
	bath	700 x 1700	1	1	1	1	1	1	1
	wash hand basin	600 x 400	1	1	1	1	1	1	1
Optional	shower tray	750 x 750							
Separate toilet	WC + cistern				1	1	1	1	1
	cloakroom basin				1	1	1	1	1

	1 bed, 1-2 person flat	2 bed, 3 person flat	2 bed, 3 person house	2 bed, 4 person house	3 bed, 5 person flat	3 bed, 5 person house	3 bed, 5 person house	3 bed, 5 person flat	4 bed, 6 person flat	4 bed, 6 person house	4 bed, 6 person house
London Housing Design Guide	50 sqm	61 sqm		70 sqm	83 sqm	86 sqm	96 sqm	102 sqm	99 sqm	107 sqm	113 sqm
No. of storeys	1	1		1	2	1	2	3	1	2	3
HCA Proposed Core Housing Design Standards	48 sqm	61 sqm	71 sqm	70 sqm	80 sqm	86 sqm	96 sqm	101 sqm	99 sqm	109 sqm	114 sqm
No. of Storeys	1	1	2	1	2	1	2	3	1	2	3
Lifetime Homes Meeting Part M			71-76 sqm				74 sqm	82 sqm			118-120 sqm
No. of Storeys			2				2	3			3
English Partnership 2007	51 sqm	66 sqm	66 sqm	77 sqm	93 sqm		66 sqm	106 sqm			
No. of Storeys	1	1	1	1	1		1	1			
National Housing Federation 2008	50 sqm	61 sqm		70 sqm	82 sqm	86 sqm	96 sqm	102 sqm	108 sqm	114 sqm	
No. of Storeys	1	1		1	2	1	2	3	2	3	
Housing Quality Indicator 2003	45-50 sqm	57-67 sqm		67-75 sqm	75-85 sqm	82-85 sqm		85-95 sqm	95-100 sqm	100-105 sqm	
No. of Storeys	1	1		1	1	2		1	2	3	
Parker Morris 1961	45.5 sqm	57.8 sqm		73.8 sqm	80.7 sqm	84.1 sqm	96.1 sqm	87.8 sqm	94.2 sqm	99.8 sqm	
No. of Storeys	1	1		2	1	2	3	1	2	3	

Notes:

1- All figures are internal floor area in square metres.

2- Housing Quality Indicator areas exclude external storage

3- Parker Morris include an allowance for internal storage

(Left) Table 4.4
Living Space Furniture Schedule -
London Housing Design Guide / mae Architects 2009

(Above) Table 4.5
Housing internal area comparison

5. Case Study - Typical Terrace House

Case Study

With life expectancy rising it is becoming a stronger possibility that residents will spend even longer periods of their life in the home. This development will generate new needs and thus place demands on both the existing dwellings of such residents and on any newly constructed housing. As residents desire to remain within their home (a recognisable environment), care will increasingly take place in the domestic environment.

It is not enough to merely fulfill construction specification norms such as wider doors, sufficient space to manoeuvre a wheelchair and zimmer frame. Increasingly, additional demands must be addressed and fulfilled relating to the psychology of dwelling and social integration.

In addition to the electronic future proofing issues with regards building in accordance with the needs of elderly are:

-Adapting existing housing to meet the needs economically.

-Planning and building new dwellings with particular regard for the later years of life.

-Considering residential forms in which young people can live with seniors, or seniors with each other.

Different residential possibilities entail a number of considerations about the future floor plan so that the given conditions can be fulfilled:

-Functional connections between bedrooms, sanitary areas and storage space must be considered very carefully to make barrier free care possible in the home.

-It should be possible to combine rooms that become free after the children have moved out. Could this set up a rental opportunity to supplement a less than opulent pension? Or provide accommodation for a care worker?

Addition consideration should also be given to the kind of surroundings suited to the needs of the elderly.

-Public transport connections should be located nearby.

-Services for the elderly, day hospitals, day care should be in the vicinity.

-And it also means that opportunities for social interaction can take place at a café, supermarket and post office in the area.

Terrace house adaptions
Historically alterations made within the domestic environment generally ranged from decorative improvements, new fixtures and fitting to an existing kitchen or bathroom, the merging of rooms (living and dining) and house extensions carried out following advice from a friendly builder. This range of home improvements were generally undertaken without tackling the requirements for future ground floor WC/bathroom, reduced thresholds and general improvements for greater accessibility around the home.

Conversion or improvement of ground floor lean-to building at the rear of the house from an external store/pantry adapted into a new kitchen space. This allows for the existing kitchen to become the dining space accessed directly by the kitchen and not via a corridor/hallway.

Following the new location of the dining room the back room and living room were usually knocked through in to one large living room. The old dining space could become a third bedroom, with new WC located under the staircase.

Porch/main entrance, moved forward to the front façade creating a lobby arrangement, which might have increased the thermal capacity of the GF hall area. However, this (intern) creates a difficult configuration process for the infirm or those wheelchair bound.

Typical Terrace House
Taking a typical early 1900's terrace house as a model for an ALIP adaptable home. The Plan below shows the property in its current existing layout, and the Plans over show the possible adapted arrangements for the occupiers caring needs within this housing type.

Figure 5.1
Existing Terrace House - Ground & First Floor Plan (NTS)

Proposed Adaptions

There have been 6 main physical changes to the plan form.

1 -Entrance lobby arrangement.
2 -Hallway / circulation to ground & first floor.
3 -Ground floor WC inserted below staircase.
4 -Staircase re-configured.
5 -Open plan kitchen / dining area.
6 -Connection between bedroom and bathroom.

These changes to the building fabric allow the home to be adapted for use by a number of end users ranging from independent users with occasional carer support through to a live-in carer / nurse.

Figure 5.2
Proposed Terrace House (Option 1)
Ground & First Floor Plan (NTS)

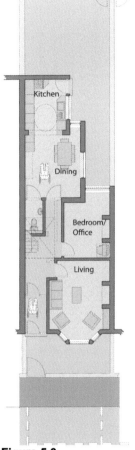

Figure 5.3
Proposed Terrace House (Option 2)
Ground & First Floor Plan (NTS)

External Spaces

A provision for distinctive clues to enable wayfinding to assist orientation within developments needs to be included, particularly where an element of repetition of the dwellings has been designed. The wayfinding clues should range from distinctive trees, street furniture and scented planting.

Pavements

Surfaces should be smooth, even and slip resistant. Consideration must be given for the potential settlement of below ground materials when incorporating abutment surfaces and joints. Footpath edges should have a distinctive or contrasting kerb line.

Street Furniture

When considering the placement of street furniture within a development, the location should be situated to provide visual landmarks. Furniture needs to be set back from the footpath without causing potential hazards.

Planting

The choice of planting is to be selected to assist wayfinding and positioned in proximity to street furniture or building entrances as natural forms of signposting around developments. Colour, aroma, distinctive forms and even texture of planting will all assist as directional landmarks, however provision must be taken to ensure an adequate maintenance programme is adopted to prevent planting from overhanging footpaths.

On Street Parking

Where designated On-street parking bays are provided they should be sited where road gradients and camber are reasonably level, e.g. 1:50. A dropped kerb (with blister paving), or level surface should be provided to permit convenient access.

In communal parking situations good practice would recommend that at least one parking space within each parking bay / location / lift core location have a minimum 3300mm effective clear width or be a designated accessible parking bay. Overall, 10% of parking bays / provisions should have the increased accessible dimensions. The design of the parking layout and landscaping should also enable some further parking spaces within bays to be increased in size according to demand and set out by Local Authority Planning requirements.

Adequate space should be provided to prevent vehicles parking in undesignated bays and deter cars from parking partly on the kerb and pavement.

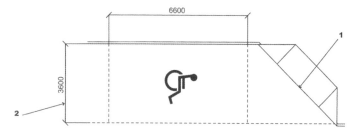

1 - Dropped kerb (with blister paving)
2 - Allows safety zone on kerb or street

Figure 5.4
On-street parking

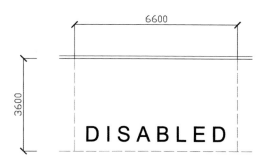

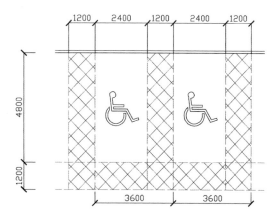

Figure 5.5
Parking bay layout and alternative On-street parking

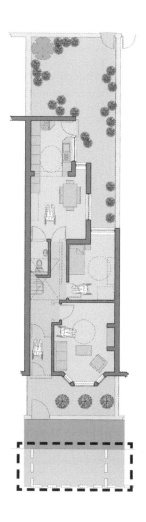

54

Access from Car Parking

The distance from the car parking space to the home should be kept to a minimum and should be level or gently sloping. Where the change in level is sufficient to avoid a single step, a stepped approach should also be provided.

Level; steeper than 1:60 (but less steep than 1:20) is gently sloping; and 1:20 or steeper is a ramp.

Where an access route has a gradient steeper than 1:60, but not as steep as 1:20, it should have a level landing for each 500 mm rise of the access route. A level landing should also be provided wherever a change of direction occurs.

A maximum gradient of 1:12 is permissible on an individual slope of less than 5 metres or 1:15 if it is between 5 and 10m, and 1:20 where it is more than 10m.

Paths should be a minimum of 900mm wide.

Footway and Footpath Material

An access route should have a firm, slip-resistant and reasonably smooth surface. Cobbles, bare earth, sand and unbonded gravel should not be used.

Private external areas

Main entrances to either the front or rear of the dwelling should maintain level (or suitably graded), access between external and internal areas providing accessible communal garden spaces to all.

Clear delineation of private, semi-private and public is required to all dwelling boundaries. Pathways and entrance pathways should be distinguishable during the day and night.
A variation in materials should be considered between the boundary walls and entrance gates to enforce the wayfinding strategy.

Limits for ramp gradients		
Going of a flight	Maximum gradient	Maximum rise
10m	1:20	500mm
9m	1:19	473mm
8m	1:18	444mm
7m	1:17	411mm
6m	1:16	375mm
5m	1:15	333mm
4m	1:14	285mm
3m	1:13	230mm
Not exceeding 2m	1:12	166mm

Table 5.1
Gradient of a Ramp - BS 8300: 2009

Main entrance to dwelling

Lighting
A good spread of light levels along all entrance paths should be provided at night with an increase in lux levels at the entrance vestibule. Secondary paths around the dwelling or developments should be allocated PIR sensor activated security lighting.

Entrances to dwellings
A contrast in materials and colours between main entrance doors in multi tenancy developments should be adopted in a similar approach to the external gateways and boundary walls, this will assist in wayfinding.

Some degree of weather protection at the entrance door will be required, providing some element of shelter for rest and key location for opening the door. Support posts or structures should not provide obstacles to circulation routes towards the entrance door.

Provisions for the future proofing of the entrance area should be accommodated in terms of both the building fabric and retrofitting supportive electronic devises. Capped off electrics for the provision of door opening equipment, video and key fob entrance systems should be provided.

Confined internal entrance vestibules can prove difficult spaces for maneuvering in wheelchairs or when entering with shopping, in order to alleviate further problems it is imperative that a level detail between internal and external thresholds and entrance mat wells is consistent. All entrance doors should have a minimum clear opening width of 800mm.

Allow for the potential use of natural light into the entrance. Consideration of high gloss paint finishes or highly reflective materials should be avoided as these material finishes can cause confusion. An understanding of the residents needs and abilities must be taken into account.

Where the change in level is less than 300mm, a ramp is the only viable means of access, as it avoids the need for a single step.

Ensure that any matting provided within communal entrances has its surface level with adjacent floor finish or, if surface laid, has chamfered edges that are not a vertical up-stand barrier and will not fray to become a trip hazard.

Access Ironmongery
A handrail with an oval profile should have dimensions of 50mm wide and 38mm deep. The profile should have rounded edges with a radius of at least 15 mm. Any circular handrail should have a diameter of between 32 mm and 45 mm.

There should be a clearance of between 60 mm and 75 mm between a handrail and any adjacent wall surface, and any handrail support should meet the handrail, centrally, on its underside. The clearance between the bottom of the rail and any cranked support, or continuous balustrade, should be at least 50 mm to minimize the risk of the handrail supports interrupting the smooth running of a person's hand along the rail.

Ironmongery

Door entry systems and door bells should be set so that controls are in a zone 1000mm – 1200mm from the floor and within 200mm of the door frame on the latch side.

Entrance doors to a building should be usable by disabled people even though they might be designed to be held closed when not in use.

Consider providing a nib on the push side of entrance doors of min. 200mm on the latch side (in addition to the minimum 300mm nib on the pull side).

All ironmongery should be effortless and comfortable during operation. Door handles should be lever or 'D' type in accordance with the locking requirements and/or the specific needs of the resident.

Ironmongery should meet the needs of the above whilst avoiding the associated stigma of a special care environment.

The opening method of doors and their associated ironmongery should be consistent throughout the property.

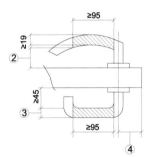

a) Lever handles returned towards the door for solid doors and those with side margins of 100mm or wider.

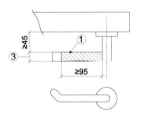

b) Cranked lever handle for solid doors and those with side margins of 100mm or wider.

Key

1- Hand grip zone (shaded) of at least 95mm (applies to all types of lever handle).

2 - Hand grip zone of at least 45mm from face of door.

3. Lever diameter at least 19mm.

4. Lock/latch backset at least 54mm from door edge.

5. Reduced lock/latch backset to suit narrow stile.

6. Start of hand grip zone at least 63.5mm set back from door edge.

NOTE: Lever designs are indicative only.

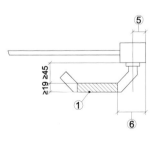

c) Lever handle designed for use with a door having a narrow stile less than 100mm wide.

Figure 5.6
Examples of Lever Furniture - BS 8300: 2009

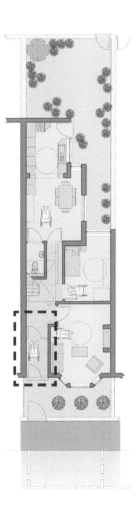

Living Areas

Where possible layouts should avoid forced and fixed furniture positions, consideration must be given to window and internal door location into the room, perimeter layout of furniture maybe preferred. Spaces within a living room less than 3000mm should be avoided, however if a narrow space cannot be avoided this area could be utilised for a home office area.

Radiators should be located where they discourage a reasonable and flexible layout. Electrical sockets must not be located within 750mm of an internal corner. Consideration should be given when planning the location of sockets for the reading, writing and eating within the room.

The provision of a through-floor lift must identified within the room and taken into account. Following the location of this zone the first floor construction will need to incorporate floor trimmers within the floor zone for future adaption's between the living area and bedroom or allocated room on the first floor.

Space standards

Designers should ensure that adequate space is provided for efficient circulation routes within all communal and dwellings spaces. A furniture layout indicating a potential fixtures and fittings layout should be provided for all rooms ensuring all spaces are clear of obstacles and hazards.

Designers should also be aware that furniture, be it for a bedroom, dining or living area come in a multitude of styles, sizes and forms. Therefore careful consideration must be taken on the shape of the room and the openings into which residents, furniture and equipment will be positioned.

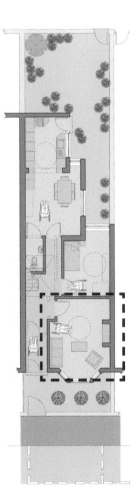

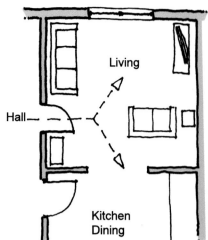

Figure 5.7
Example of Internal movement path

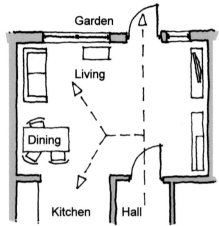

Figure 5.8
Example of Internal movement path

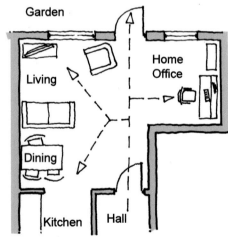

Figure 5.9
Example of Internal movement path

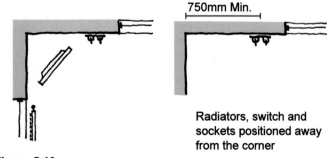

Figure 5.10
Fixtures, Switches and Sockets positioning

Access Stair Lift

Due to the configuration of the existing staircase in this example a staircase chair lift would not be a practical solution given the number of landings configured on the staircase.

A convenient bedroom can be provided within the existing study room with a stair lift providing access to the first floor bathroom.

Stairs within dwellings
Stairs should maintain a clear width of 900mm from the wall to the inside edge of the handrail.

The stair should have capped off electrics for the future inclusion of a stair lift.

Polished or slippery surfaces should be avoided for use on the stair treads and landings.

A consistent design approach is to be undertaken across all staircases within large developments containing numerous stairs.

Where possible natural light should be maximized to the stairwell, however direct light from rising or setting sun should be controlled from an East or West direction.

Artificial lighting to the staircase must be accessed via switches positioned at the top and bottom of the staircase. The artificial lighting of the staircase when switched on, should reach adequate lux levels.

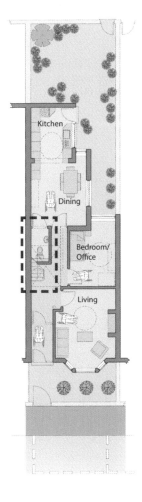

Bedrooms and Mobility hoists

Is it possible to find a variety of beds which can also serve as hospital beds should stationary care become necessary as the resident ages or their condition declines?

What about the surroundings of a bed where the resident has to spend more time.

-Can the occupant see who is at the front door when the bell rings?

-Is it possible to turn on a pivot screen television screen whilst lying in the bed?

-Can a laptop also be used there comfortably?

-Can the window be open or closed when the occupant is about to fall asleep?

-Is it possible to eat comfortably in bed?

-Can the lighting be adapted to the occupant's reading habits?

Ensure that the bedroom has sufficient space for the usual furniture items whilst allowing for the manoeuvrability of those requiring assistance from wheelchairs entering the room and getting in and out of bed.

Capped off electrical sockets should be provided to all bedrooms to allow for the future installation of hoists, with the possibility of the track extending from the bedroom to the bathroom. The retro fitting of a hoist system depending on the users requirements could necessitate the strengthening of ceiling joists depending on the construction of the dwelling.

Should the bathroom be located next to the bedroom then a knock out wall panel between the two rooms should be considered when designing the development.

Electrical provision should be considered for TV, FM aerial, internet access, telephone and phone entry systems. Furniture layouts are to be developed to ensure the future flexibility of the bedrooms.

Mobility Hoists

Fixed Mobility Hoist
The disabled mobility hoist is ideally suited for home use, especially in homes where characteristics, such as small bathrooms, narrow hallways and doors etc., hinder the use of a mobile hoist. The mobility hoist is lightweight and easy to set up and take down. Several supports can be positioned around the home and the hoist transferred between them making it suitable for transfers between wheelchair and bed, bath and chair. Weight 17.7kg.

Portable Mobility Hoist
The mobility hoist is an ideal choice for paediatrics' due to the reduced dimensions. It is also excellent for use in small houses or where space is restricted. The mobility hoist is lightweight and dismantles into two parts for storage and transportation. High stability, along with the correct sling choice, allows it to lift a person from the floor. A pedal system is used to open the legs of the base to facilitate use. Weight 29.3kg.

Bathrooms
With regard to sanitary and cooking facilities a number of products are readily available. However grip holds and shower seats to simplify personal hygiene routine of the elderly are not enough. When undertaking the refurbishment of bathrooms to suit the needs specific to the user it is imperative when ensuring the water tightness of the wet room construction.

-Adjustable toilet bowls can be difficult to source.

-Bath tubs are still cemented to the building with the disadvantage that their removal requires disproportionate cost and effort.

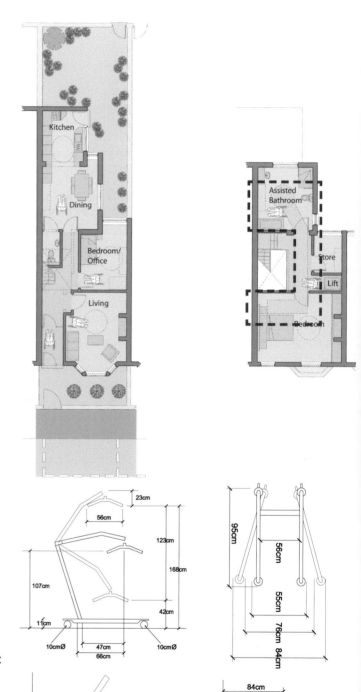

Figure 5.11
Portable mobility hoists - www.independentliving.co.uk

60

Hallways and Storage

Corridors and passageways in the entrance storey should be sufficiently wide to allow convenient circulation by a wheelchair user. Consideration should be given to the effects of local obstruction such as radiators and other fixtures.

Hallways and circulation routes should be as simple as possible. If possible the clear width set out at the entrance area should be a continuous clear width throughout the dwelling. Corridors and the connected doorways must enable access to people with different degrees of mobility.

All doors on entrance level should maintain a 300mm nib wall to the leading edge, preventing the leading edge being tight into the corner of a room. Doors should not open out into hallways.

Potential fixed objects such as radiators, within circulation routes should be designed out to facilitate greater movement and mobility.

A requirement for a well lit storage space in the vicinity of the main entrance should be considered to house large bulky item such as a pram, wheelchair or bicycle, recessed off the main corridor. Storage should be available to prevent a cluttered and less hazardous space.

Storage
600mm deep wardrobes layout and design can be cumbersome. Raised foot plate make it impossible for walk in wheelchair access in to the wardrobe

Storage spaces, be they bedroom, bathroom cabinets or furniture in the hallways can generally still be built up to 2.3m high with the consequence that things are located too high.They can only be accessed via a foot stool or step ladder, that leads to a potential fall risk. This can also apply to bookshelves.

When sight fails, hearing, memory and mobility become reduced; when the directions and distances a person can reach change or muscle strength ebbs these conditions need not mean that an independent, safe and comfortable life in ones own home is no longer possible.

Collaboration among architects, interior designers and industrial designers work together, it would be possible to develop a consciousness for building in accordance with the needs of the elderly.

Doorway clear opening width (mm)	Corridor / passageway width (mm)
750 or wider	900 (when approach head-on)
750	1200 (when approach not head-on)
775	1050 (when approach not head-on)
800	900 (when approach not head-on)

Table 5.2
Minimum widths of corridors and passageways for a range of doorway widths - the building regulations, Part M

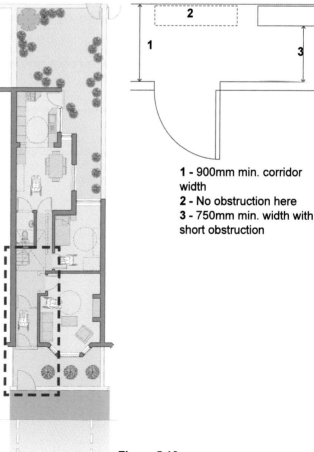

1 - 900mm min. corridor width
2 - No obstruction here
3 - 750mm min. width with short obstruction

Figure 5.12
Corridors, passages and internal doors
- the building regulations, Part M

Doors Switches and Sockets

Switches, sockets and service controls should be at a height usable by all (i.e. between 450mm and 1200mm from the floor). Provide capped off electrical outlets or fused spurs at relevant locations to assist simple, cost effective provision of the future possible adaptations:

Stair lift.
Through floor lift.
Automatic window controls for inaccessible windows in kitchens and bathrooms.

Hoist between bedroom and bathroom.

Task lighting under kitchen wall cupboards if not already installed.

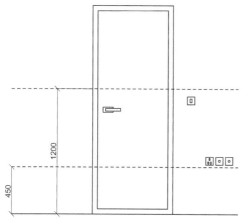

Figure 5.13
Heights of switches and sockets - the building regulations, Part M

Windows
Living room window glazing should begin at 800mm or lower and windows must be easy to open/operate.

With glazing at an appropriate level, people can enjoy the views through the window whilst seated.

Wheelchair users must be able to open at least one window in each room.

Where possible, capped off electrical sockets should be provided to all windows for the future installation of mechanically operated blinds and assisted windows opening mechanism.

Location of window controls and reach limitations for wheelchair users

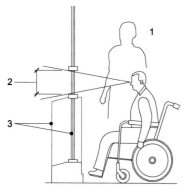

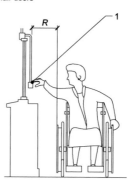

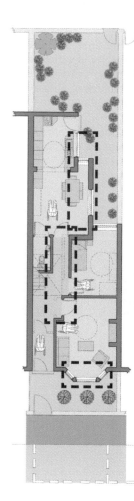

Key
1. Transom height chosen to allow a view through window
2. No transom between 800 and 1200 above floor level
3. Wall or opaque infill panel

Figure 5.14
Height of window transoms allowing a view from a wheelchair or chair - BS8300

Key
1. Manual or powered controls between 800mm and 1000mm above floor level

Max. reach *R* :
- 400mm at 90° to window
- 360mm at 60° to window

Access Circulation and Thresholds

Maintain level access across the entrance level.

The guidance has been re-written to clarify that the cumulative height of the threshold, including an upstand, is 15mm. An upstand of more than 5mm high should be chamfered or pencil rounded.

Hard surfaces can cause sound reverberation and increased background noise levels, which can cause difficulties for people with hearing impairments. A mixture of hard and soft surfaces should be used.

Carpets should be of shallow dense pile. Avoid coir matting, deep pile or excessively grooved carpets to allow easy passage for wheelchair users.

Junctions between different flooring materials should be carefully detailed so as not to create an obstacle to wheelchair users or a trip hazard for people with mobility or visual impairment. Mat wells incorporated into the entrance hallway should be of a standard size allowing for ease of future replacement.

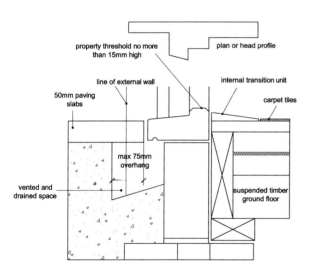

Figure 5.15
External Threshold Detail

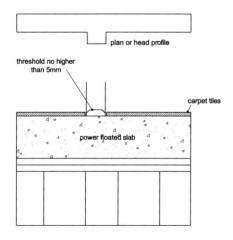

Figure 5.16
Internal Threshold Detail

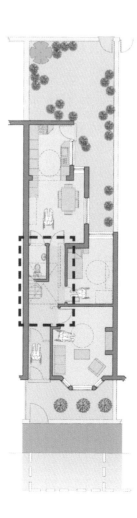

Kitchen

There are accessible kitchens but the electrical systems used to adjust the worktops or equipment drives up their cost. Therefore should such devices need to be controlled mechanically at all? Consideration is to be given when planning kitchen layouts for the specific needs of the end user.

-Is the standard height 850-940mm acceptable?

-Can the resident use the worktop whilst seated?

-Is an adjustable worktop suitable?

Dwellings and care environments focusing on specific needs can provide greater activity for residents and visitors interaction especially in the form a kitchen–living room as living space; here is where the socializing tasks can be preformed.

The location of controls and sockets in relation to specified appliances should be considered. Controls should be suitable for a range of people, including those with limited dexterity. The incorporation of task lighting below wall cupboards should be considered in addition to the main room lighting.

Unobstructed space or knee recess at least 600mm wide provided to one side of the kitchen appliances.

The extent to which knee recesses can be provided will depend on the amount of floor-mounted cupboard space required. The side on which a knee recess is located is determined by the handing of the appliance doors and controls.

Variable height work surfaces for self-contained / self catering accommodation designed for disabled people. Changeable work surface between 750mm – 900mm. Storage units and services to sinks should also be adjustable with storage units provided as mobile units.

Work surface no greater than a depth of 600mm.

Where a kitchen area suitable for wheelchair users and ambulant disabled people is provided in a building, it should be located on an accessible route that is direct and obstruction-free. See figure 5.16.

Operation of all hot and cold water taps should be suitable for people with limited hand dexterity, e.g. quarter turn simple lever taps. The form of taps and method of tap control should be consistent throughout the dwelling to suit the specific needs and requirements of the occupant.

The kitchen layout should maximize the number of tasks possible from a single advantageous location, reducing excessive manouvering. The preferred layout should allow for the use of multiple areas whilst avoiding cross routes between areas either side of the kitchen.

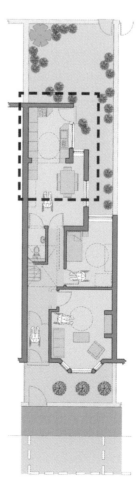

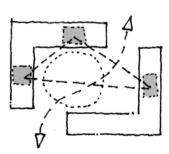

Figure 5.17
Inefficient kitchen layout. Circulation routes and kitchen layout create potential circulation clashes

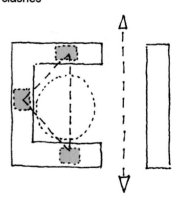

Figure 5.18
Efficient kitchen layout with no circulation clashes

New and Future Technology

Intelligent Floors
Floor sensors alarm you when movement is not detected, when a person goes to bed or gets out of bed, as well as if they have fallen. Providing power. Automatically illuminate at night.

WC
Using the toilet is a part of everyday life. The role of the toilet has long been limited to flushing away waste, but that may be about to change with hi-tech intelligent systems. Analyse the colour, consistency and odour of your waste to give you dietary advice. Send the results directly to your doctor if necessary. Measures the user's blood pressure, weight, body fat, and urine sugar level, the results are wirelessly sent to your PC, where you can plot all your personal statistics on graphs and charts.

Flupper
Flupper is a human powered system for moving between floors yet, it requires less than 10% of the effort compared to stairs. Proven in a study with the Biodynamics Department of Imperial College / Charing Cross Hospital. Flupper: 3.6m in < 8sec - stairs: 3.6m in > 17sec.

This means that many of those unable to take stairs can use flupper.

Figure 5.19
Intelligent floor

Figure 5.20
Intelligent WC

Figure 5.21
Flupper - Rombout Frieling. Royal College of Art
www.flupper.to

Physical

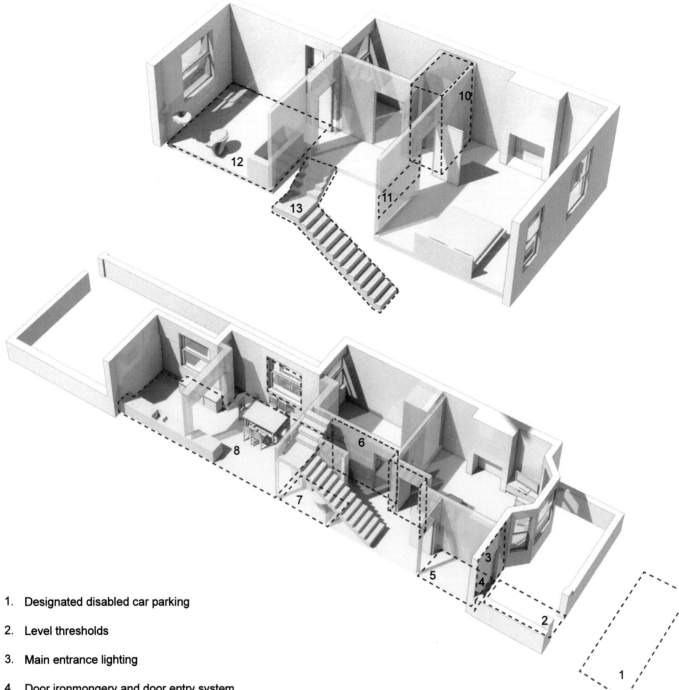

1. Designated disabled car parking

2. Level thresholds

3. Main entrance lighting

4. Door ironmongery and door entry system

5. Appropriate lobby arrangement

6. Physical adaption to accommodate wheelchair access to hallway
    and all doors

7. Ground floor WC

8. Kitchen adapted to suit needs of home user

9. Window controls for wheelchair users

10. Through floor vertical movement systems

11. Switches and sockets

12. Bathroom adaptable for hoist access to suit user and future
    needs

13. Staircase adapted to accommodate stair lift

Technology

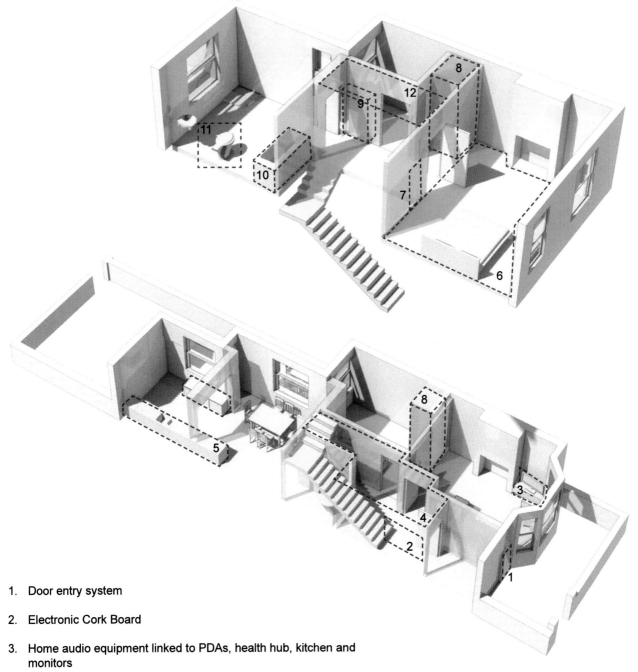

1. Door entry system

2. Electronic Cork Board

3. Home audio equipment linked to PDAs, health hub, kitchen and monitors

4. PIR sensors to detect and develop users daily living patterns around the home

5. Height-adjustable kitchen units. Intelligent work surface. Kitchen white goods and cookers connected into home electronic system

6. Intelligent floor and bed to detect falls and movements in habitable rooms

7. Household lighting linked to PDA

8. 'Flupper' vertical walking

9. Central location for home hub technology

10. Bath linked to PDA

11. WC linked to health hub

12. Ambient light levels linked to PIR sensors to aid nighttime movement through the home.

6. Digital Connectivity
& Remote Control

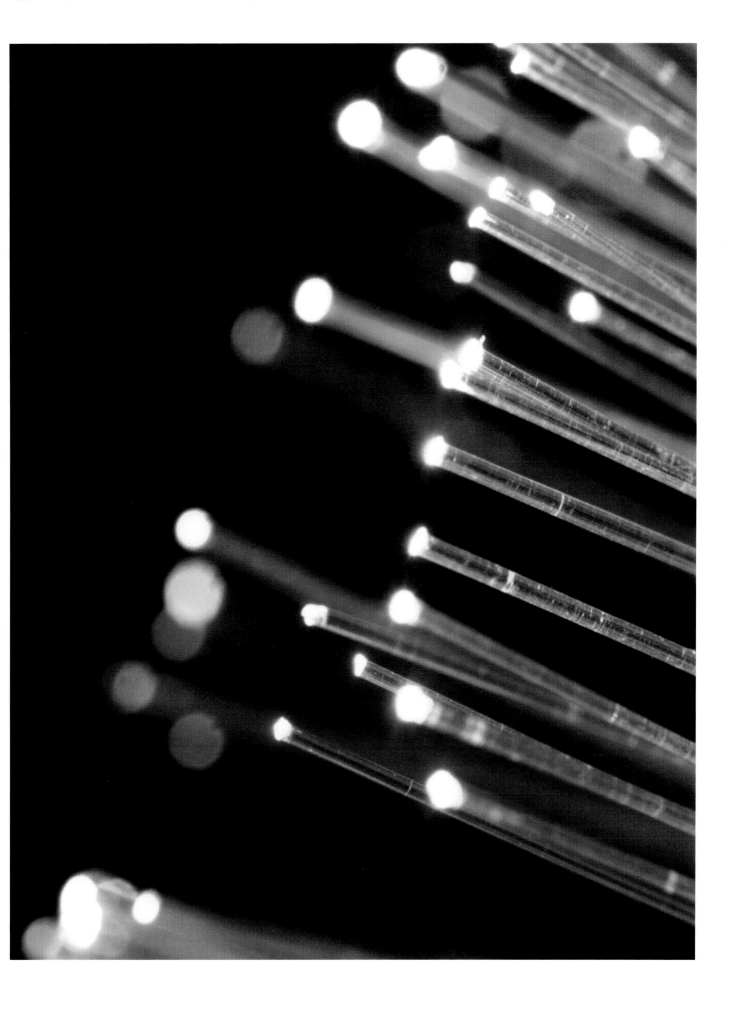

Overview and Benefits

As the amount of controllable fittings and domestic appliances in the home rises, the ability of these devices to interconnect and communicate with each other digitally becomes a useful and desirable feature. The consolidation of control or monitoring signals from appliances, fittings or basic services is an aim of home automation.

In simple installations this may be as straightforward as turning on the lights when a person enters the room. In advanced installations, rooms can sense not only the presence of a person inside but know who that person is and perhaps set appropriate lighting, temperature, music levels or television channels, taking into account the day of the week, the time of day, and other factors.

Other automated tasks may include setting the air conditioning to an energy saving setting when the building is unoccupied, and restoring the normal setting when an occupant is about to return. More sophisticated systems can maintain an inventory of products, recording their usage through a Radio-frequency identification (RFID) tag, and prepare a shopping list or even automatically order replacements.

Home automation can also provide a remote interface to home appliances or the automation system itself, via telephone line, wireless transmission or the internet, to provide control and monitoring via a Smart Phone or Web browser.

An example of a remote monitoring implementation of home automation could be when a smoke detector detects a fire or smoke condition, then all lights in the house will blink to alert any occupants of the house to the possible fire. If the house is equipped with a home theatre, a home automation system can shut down all audio and video components to display the alert or make an audible announcement. The system could also call the home owner on their mobile phone to alert them, or call the fire brigade or alarm monitoring company to bring it to their attention.

Standards and Bridges

There have been many attempts to standardise the forms of hardware, electronic and communication interfaces needed to construct a home automation system. Specific domestic wiring and communication standards include:

BACnet

INSTEON

X10

KNX (standard)

LonWorks

C-Bus

SCS BUS with OpenWebNet

Universal Powerline Bus

ZigBee and,

Z-wave

Some standards use additional communication and control wiring, some embed signals in the existing power circuit of the house, some use radio frequency (RF) signals, and some use a combination of several methods. Control wiring is hardest to retrofit into an existing house. Some appliances include USB that is used to control it and connect it to a domestic network. Bridges translate information from one standard to another (eg. from X10 to European Installation Bus).

Tasks

Heating, Ventilation and Air Conditioning (HVAC)

HVAC solutions include temperature and humidity control. This is generally one of the most important aspects to a homeowner. An Internet-controlled thermostat, for example, can both save money and help the environment, by allowing the homeowner to control the building's heating and air conditioning systems remotely.

Lighting

Lighting control systems can be used to control household electric lights in a variety of ways:

Extinguish all the lights of the house.

Replace manual switching with automation of on and off signals for any or all lights.

Regulation of electric illumination levels according to the level of ambient light available.

Change the ambient colour of lighting via control of LEDs or electronic dimmers.

Natural lighting

Natural lighting control involves controlling window shades, LCD shades, draperies and awnings. Recent advances include use of RF technology to avoid wiring to switches and integration with third party home automation systems for centralised control.

Audio

This category includes audio switching and distribution. Audio switching determines the selection of an audio source. Audio distribution allows an audio source to be heard in one or more rooms. This feature is often referred to as 'multi-zone' audio.

The components that allow audio throughout your home, or business:

CAT 5e/ CAT6 cable from a central audio unit.

Security

Control and integration of security systems.

With 'Home Automation', the consumer can select and watch cameras live from an Internet source to their home or business. Security cameras can be controlled, allowing the user to observe activity around a house or business right from a monitor or touch panel. Security systems can include motion sensors that will detect any kind of unauthorised movement and notify the user through the security system or via a mobile phone.

This category also includes control and distribution of security cameras (see surveillance).

Detection of possible intrusion.
Sensors of detection of movement.

Sensors of magnetic contact of door/window.

Sensors of glass breaking.

Sensors of pressure changes.

Simulation of presence.

Detection of fire, gas leaks, water leaks (see fire alarm and gas alarm).

Medical alert. Teleassistance.

Precise and safe closing of blinds/curtains.

Intercoms
An intercom system allows communication via a microphone and loud speaker between multiple rooms.

Ubiquity in the external control via internal, remote control from the Internet, PC, wireless controls (PDA with Wi-Fi), electrical equipment.

Transmission of alarms.

Intercommunications.

Other systems
Using special hardware, almost any device can be monitored and controlled automatically or remotely, including:

Coffee pot

Garage door

Pet feeding and watering

Plant watering

Different methods and standards of wireless communication have developed across the world, based on various commercially driven requirements. These technologies can roughly be classified into four individual categories, based on their specific application and transmission range. These categories are summarised in the figure 6.1. and are expanded below.

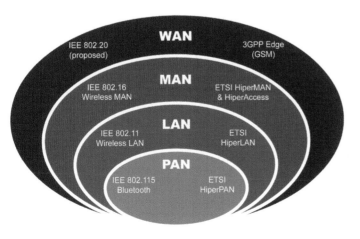

Figure 6.1
Global Wireless Standards

Personal Area Network (PAN)
A Personal Area Network (PAN) is a computer network used for communication among computer devices (including telephones and personal digital assistants) close to one person. The reach of a PAN is typically a few metres. PAN's can be used for communication among the personal devices themselves (intrapersonal communication), or for connecting to a higher level network and the Internet.

Personal area networks may be wired with computer buses such as USB and FireWire. However, a Wireless Personal Area Network (WPAN) is made possible with network technologies such as Infrared (IrDA) and Bluetooth.

Bluetooth
Bluetooth is an industrial specification for wireless personal area networks (PANs), also known as IEEE 802.15.1. Bluetooth provides a way to connect and exchange information between devices such as personal digital assistants (PDAs), mobile phones, laptops, PCs, printers, digital cameras and video game consoles via a secure, globally unlicensed short-range radio frequency.

Bluetooth is a radio standard and communications protocol primarily designed for low power consumption, with a short range (power class dependent: 1 metre, 10 metres, 100 metres) based around low-cost transceiver microchips in each device.

Figure 6.2
Local area network

Infrared (IrDA)
The Infrared Data Association (IrDA) defines physical specifications communications protocol standards for the short range exchange of data over infrared light, for typical use in Personal Area Networks.

Local Area Network (LAN)
A wireless LAN or WLAN is a wireless Local Area Network, which is the linking of two or more computers without using wires. It uses radio communication to accomplish the same functionality that a wired LAN has. WLAN utilises spread-spectrum technology based on radio waves to enable communication between devices in a limited area, also known as the basic service set. This gives users the mobility to move around within a broad coverage area and still be connected to the network. IEEE 802.11

IEEE 802.11, the Wi-Fi standard, denotes a set of wireless LAN/WLAN standards developed by working group 11 of the IEEE LAN/MAN Standards Committee (IEEE 802). The 802.11 family currently includes six over-the-air modulation techniques that all use the same protocol. The most popular (and prolific) techniques are those defined by the b, a, and g amendments to the original standard. The adjacent table summarises the different 802.11 standards:

Protocol	Release Date	Op. Frequency	Data Rate (Typical)	Data Rate (Max)	Range (Indoor)
Legacy	1997	2.4 - 2.5 GHz	1 Mbit/s	2 Mbit/s	?
802.11a	1999	5.15-5.35/5.47-5.725/5.725-5.875 GHz	25 Mbit/s	54 Mbit/s	~30 meters (~100 feet)
802.11b	1999	2.4-2.5 GHz	6.5 Mbit/s	11 Mbit/s	~50 meters (~150 feet)
802.11g	2003	2.4-2.5 GHz	11 Mbit/s	54 Mbit/s	~30 meters (~100 feet)
802.11n	2006 (draft)	2.4 GHz or 5 GHz bands	200 Mbit/s	540 Mbit/s	~50 meters (~160 feet)

Table 6.1
Fequency development

Metropolitan Area Network (MAN)
Wireless Metropolitan Area Network (MAN) is the name trademarked by the IEEE 802.16 Working Group on Broadband Wireless Access Standards for its wireless metropolitan area network standard (commercially known as WiMAX), which defines broadband Internet access from fixed or mobile devices via antennas. Subscriber stations communicate with base-stations that are connected to a core network. This is a good alternative to fixed line networks and it is simple to build and relatively inexpensive.

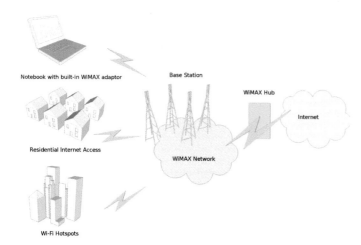

Figure 6.2
Metro Area Network image

WiMAX
WiMAX is defined as Worldwide Interoperability for Microwave Access by the WiMAX Forum, formed in June 2001 to promote conformance and interoperability of the IEEE 802.16 standard, officially known as WirelessMAN. The Forum describes WiMAX as "a standards-based technology enabling the delivery of last mile wireless broadband access as an alternative to cable and DSL".

The range of WiMAX probably generates more confusion than any other single aspect of WiMAX. It is common to see statements in the media describing WiMAX multipoint coverage extending 30 miles. In a strict technical sense (in some spectrum ranges) this is correct, with even greater ranges being possible in point to point links. In practice in the real world (and especially in the license-free bands) this is wildly overstated especially where non line of sight (NLOS) reception is concerned.

Due to a variety of factors, the average cell ranges for most WiMAX networks will likely boast 4-5 mile range (in NLOS capable frequencies) even through tree cover and building walls. Service ranges up to 10 miles (16 kilometres) are very likely in line of sight (LOS) applications (once again depending upon frequency). Ranges beyond 10 miles are certainly possible but for scalability purposes may not be desirable for heavily loaded networks. In most cases, additional cells are indicated to sustain high quality of service (QOS) capability. For the carrier class approach, especially as regards mobility, cells larger than this seem unlikely in the near future.

Wide Area Network (WAN)
A Wide Area Network or WAN is a computer network covering a broad geographical area. Contrast with personal area networks (PAN's), local area networks (LAN's) or metropolitan area networks (MAN's) that are usually limited to a room, building or campus. The largest and most well-known example of a WAN is the Internet.

WAN's are used to connect local area networks (LAN's) together, so that users and computers in one location can communicate with users and computers in other locations. Many WAN's are built for one particular organisation and are private. Others,

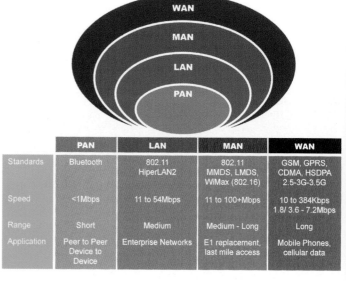

Figure 6.3
Global Wireless Standards

built by Internet service providers, provide connections from an organisation's LAN to the Internet.

In addition, WAN's also refer to Mobile Data Communications, such as GSM, GPRS and 3G. Please refer to our Mobility section for further details.

Technology Summary
These wireless communication technologies evolved over time to enable the transmission of larger amounts of data at greater speeds across a global network. Figure 6.2 on page 72 summarises the technical details of each cluster of technologies.

Wireless Technologies Overview
Essentially for projects like this we are looking at a LAN type environment. Wireless LANs operate at 2.4Ghz in accordance with the 802.11 standards, released in 1997 and currently on revision "g" allowing 54MBPS (Mega Bits Per Second) to be transmitted.

Typically most homes have a wireless router which connects to either a Cable (DSL) or telephone (ADSL) modem. The wireless repeater (usually built in to the modem) transmits the broadband signal for that property around the home, typically up to a 70 metre radius.

Signal penetration does however depend upon the physical construction of the building and the location of the wireless access point within the building. Problems can be caused by interference from water which may be piped around the house, or in older properties appears as dampness in the brickwork. 2.4Ghz is susceptible to climate related interference, as any form of water vapour may cause disruption, subsequently this does impair performance when used outside, so in practice the external applications of 2.4Ghz should be avoided.

There are several ways to get around this problem without having to run lots of cables or rely on lots of individual ADSL connections on a larger site such as a university campus or sheltered accommodation.

WiMAX Cloud
A WiMAX cloud would be ideal in an area consisting of several low lying buildings. Typically a single fibre optic Internet connection is introduced to the site and connected to a WiMAX transmitter (such as a sky pilot gateway) to provide coverage at 5.8Ghz in a radius of up to 5 miles. Each building under the cloud would require a CPE (Customer Premise Equipment) aerial which would receive the signal and provide broadband presentation via Ethernet.

A WiMAX cloud is not always required or indeed necessary, for example in a block of flats / tower block or small sheltered accommodation the fibre / Internet connection could be run to a single location and then distributed throughout the building.

Internal Distribution to a Building
Wireless Extenders / Access points may be fitted periodically throughout the building to generate, repeat and amplify 2.4 GHz signals. However, this requires a lot of equipment, possibility of damage, theft etc., so there are risks. Also a higher cost of ownership in terms of support and maintenance.

Leaky Feeder Cable
Originally developed for use in mines, there are several commercial / domestic applications of this product now on the market. Instead of fitting wireless units in to each home or flat, leaky feeder cable can be laid out in a building to provide 2.4Ghz access in a manner similar to a wireless repeater.

This application would be very beneficial in offices / flats / tower blocks and may be also applied to sheltered accommodation. Leaky feeder cables can be built in to cable conduits and may also be retrofitted, some consideration must be given to interference from electrical sources when routing cables.

Cable width is dependent upon cable length. The longer the run of cable, the thicker the cable needs to be. Widths vary from under 1/2" inch up to approximately 1.1/4" inches, this would have to be determined on an application by application basis

Mobile Phone Building Repeaters
One of the issues with modern offices is that the amount of insulation and finishes on exterior glass surfaces can make it difficult for all but the most powerful of mobile signals to penetrate. A way around this is to build in to the infrastructure a series of floor level mobile repeaters.

A range of products are available which may be tailored to either an individual network provider, or may cover all networks. You may also choose to transmit either just voice or voice + 3G and also specify the number of concurrent users the device can support.

Costs range from between £700 to £2,000 (2011), depending upon configuration and range / area of required coverage.

7. Guidance on Internal Connectivity and Assisted Living Solutions

Introduction

Intelligent Buildings and Smart Homes
The term 'intelligent buildings' is often used to refer to non-domestic buildings whilst the term 'smart home' is used to describe an intelligent dwelling. In general terms an 'intelligent building' is one which leverages the integration of technologies using a common communications network to provide a gamut of functions and services that is broader than that which would be achieved from the same technologies operating in isolation. The nature of the technology used in an intelligent building will depend on the purpose of the building (e.g. hospitals, schools etc.). A smart home will utilise technology with the aim of enhancing lifestyle or quality of life of the occupants.

In a smart home, services such as lighting and heating can be computer controlled to optimise comfort and minimise energy consumption. Home automation services and assistive technologies in particular can be of great benefit to the elderly and disabled, enabling them to be more independent and to live in their homes for longer, to be safer and more secure.

A smart home will include a cabling, powerline or wireless infrastructure or combinations of these to distribute the various electronic services around the home. The use of cable or wireless infrastructure is dependent on the reliability of the services required, with cable being more robust than powerline and wireless (see below).

Access to this infrastructure will be provided at appropriate locations for making connections to:

Internet / broadband connectivity to the home.

Other internal networks (e.g. healthcare / wellbeing, home automation, audio and video entertainment systems etc.)

A key element is likely to be a broadband connection, to gain access to internet-based services such as health and care, entertainment, online shopping, online banking, and online community care services and to facilitate remote monitoring and control of home systems.

Potential benefits
Intelligent buildings can offer savings in running costs in a number of ways including the following (not all applicable to smart homes):

Reducing energy use by more precise monitoring and control of the internal environment – water, heating and lighting – and matching these to requirements based on building occupancy.

Reducing the amount of waste generated through greater flexibility and closer monitoring and control of building processes, e.g. using software to reconfigure building services instead of physically re-wiring them or replacing components based on performance and serviceability criteria instead of simply the length of time they have been installed.

Reducing running costs by undergoing systems maintenance only when required rather than at predetermined intervals that take no account of actual use or performance.

Avoiding costs of equipment breakdowns or replacement through the early identification of problems, e.g. by being alerted to unexpected changes in the electrical load or temperature of equipment, thereby enabling corrective or preventative action to be taken before catastrophic failure occurs.

Reducing system replacement and upgrade costs through the use of a common communications protocol that promotes interoperability and supplier choice when purchasing new or replacement equipment.

Avoiding the need, through better location awareness of assets and equipment, to purchase or rent equipment because the existence or whereabouts of the required items is not known. This could be achieved through tagging or identifying where equipment is connected to the building network.

Reducing travel costs, and the associated cost of travel time, by enabling measures such as video conferencing, remote monitoring and data sharing.

Reducing theft and improving wellbeing through 24/7 security monitoring.

Smart homes present substantial opportunities for delivering enhanced and more cost-effective web-based and technology-based services to occupants. The benefits include:

'Digital Inclusion' – access for all to e-services and digital information.

Improved and lower cost social care and medical care.

Maintenance reporting.

Extended independent living.

Improved personal safety, security and 'peace of mind'.

Reduced energy consumption.

Flexible control of electrical devices.

'Peace of mind' services – such as being able to check the security system while away from home – along with home entertainment are two of the most appreciated features of a smart home.

Building's Communications Network or Infrastructure
Any building function or service may be provided by a stand-alone – or silo – system, and a mix of such systems may be incorporated in a building in order to offer the range of facilities required. Integrated, intelligent systems break down this silo solution culture to provide integrated, single-point control so that they are able to interact with each other to synchronise their operation and maximise efficiency and flexibility. They can then deliver overall functionality that is greater than the sum of the individual systems. Using a single network means that greater flexibility and potential cost savings can be achieved by using an approach known as 'structured cabling'. Structured cabling also offers the prospect of movement or reorganisation of equipment and personnel. Good design will also ensure that the network continues to offer the required access and flexibility to support future changes in building use.

Areas of application for the building network include:

Data communications – e.g. to communicate data from systems and controls.

Telecommunications.

Video streaming – video conferencing, security, entertainment.

The media used for the communications network itself will usually be a wired network, although wireless networks and powerline (communications over the mains supply) may also be used, or indeed combinations of all three. It is important that the communications network is capable of meeting the anticipated peak demand for bandwidth. The bandwidth required will depend on the number of systems that will be using the network and how much data each is likely to produce. For many building systems the bandwidth requirements are low, but for some systems, such as security cameras or other video distribution systems, bandwidth requirements can be very high. In this respect the choice of cable, or indeed fibre, used to create the communications network is critical. The types of cable or fibre that could be used, and their associated bandwidths, are as follows:

CAT5
Together with CAT5e (see below), this is currently the most commonly used network cable. CAT5 contains four twisted pairs of copper cable, which may be screened (ScTP) or more commonly unscreened (UTP). Suitable, in runs up to 100m, for networks with bandwidth requirements up to 100 MHz.

CAT5e
Similar to CAT5, but the 'e' indicates 'enhanced', which means the cable has met additional requirements for cross-talk.

CAT6
Similar to CAT5e, but uses higher quality materials that make this cable suitable for bandwidths up to 250 MHz in runs up to 100m.

CAT7
Similar to CAT6, but made to even higher standards enabling its use in networks with bandwidth requirements of up to 600 MHz in runs up to 100m.

Fibre Optic
Consists of sheathed and protected strands of high-purity glass that propagate light. Can be more complex to terminate and connect than copper cable, but in runs of 100m has 'virtually unlimited' bandwidth.

In order to communicate with each other over the common network, and support interoperability intelligent building systems should send and receive data using the same communications protocol. A number of 'open' protocols have been developed to facilitate this. Essentially an open protocol is available for use by any manufacturer, thus encouraging its widespread take-up. The major open protocols are described below as follows:

Internet Protocol (IP)
The most widely adopted open protocol. It has no specific owner, but is controlled by the Internet Engineering Task Force, which in turn is overseen by the Internet Society. The Internet Society is an international non-profit organisation that acts as a guide and conscience for the workings of the internet. There is no international standard that defines IP; instead, the protocol is defined by Internet Standard 5, which in turn is defined by a number of 'Requests for Comments' or RFCs – principally RFC 791. Many buildings already use an IP-based network as the basis of their corporate IT network, and significant infrastructure savings may be possible by combining this IT network with the building's communications network. There are a number of issues associated with this, however, including the security of the network and the disruption that may be caused by certain systems, such as networked CCTV, which place large amounts of data onto the network. Involvement of IT staff from the beginning of the design and planning stages may help prevent such problems. The use of IP as the communications protocol in intelligent buildings was featured in a previous BRE Information Paper.

BACnet
An open protocol standard approved by the American Society of Heating, Refrigerating and Air-Conditioning Engineers (ASHRAE) and adopted by the American National Standards Institute (ANSI) in 1995. BACnet is defined in ANSI/ASHRAE 135-2004 BACnet – A Data Communication Protocol for Building Automation and Control Networks.

KNX
An open protocol developed by the KNX Association. The KNX Association was formed in 1999 by the amalgamation of three organisations: the European Installation Bus Association (EIBA), the European Home Systems Association (EHSA) and BatiBUS Club International (BCI). The KNX protocol is defined in a number of standards including EN 50090 (Home and Building Electronic Systems (HBES))[4] and EN 13321 (Open data communication in building automation, controls and building management).

LonWorks
Based upon a protocol developed by the Echelon Corporation and is defined in a number of international standards including EN 14908 (Open data communication in building automation, controls and building management).

Sensors and Actuators that Monitor and Control the Building's Systems
Information from building sensors may be used by the building management system to monitor and control conditions within the building so that they are maintained within pre-determined limits. For example, sensors that monitor factors such as local temperature, humidity, lighting and room occupancy will send appropriate data, via the building's communications network, to the monitoring and control system. Here the measured conditions will be compared with the reference conditions for the specific location, and where these fall outside acceptable limits the building management systems will send instructions to the actuators of the appropriate building systems to bring the local conditions back within requirements. Other sensors may activate specific building systems in response to a change in local conditions. For example, a motion detector may indicate someone is in an area that should be unoccupied, leading to an alarm being triggered.

Building systems
There are many different types of building system that may be integrated to produce an intelligent building. Precisely what mix of systems is included will be determined by the intended use of the building. The focus of this document is on systems that support people to live independently in their homes. This includes those providing care and health support. BRE IP13/08 Part 1 also provides a number of other categories these include:

Energy use (monitoring and management).

Environmental control (e.g. temperature, humidity, lighting).

Communications.

Security and access control.

Life-safety systems.

Systems monitoring and maintenance.

Lifts and escalators.

Entertainment, Public services, and education services also need to be covered.

Connectivity to the home
Data services are currently delivered in a variety of ways including:

Standard telephony services infrastructure.

Cable television networks.

Dedicated broadband network.

Mobile telephones, wireless and satellite (especially in areas that cannot access other services).

Powerline communications technology. This is being considered for the provision of assisted living technologies to locations that may not be economic using other approaches. This technology will take advantage of existing electrical wiring to provide a range of telecommunications services to homes and communities without relying on the availability of specialised cabling.

At present it is common for digital services to be accessed within a dwelling from a single point of entry, usually an ADSL connection using copper wires (other delivery media can be used (e.g. cable, satellite etc.) The digital signal is received by an ADSL modem. Following this is a 'home hub' – i.e. a residential gateway combining the functions of a router, switch, wireless access point and firewall. The home hub distributes the digital signal throughout the home.

Broadband Availability
At present access to broadband connectivity in the UK is about 68% although the UK government has an objective to provide universal access across the UK. Access is most limited in rural areas.

External Connection Point
For existing homes the entry point for the external cable will be fixed. However, for new build there may be a choice of entry points. CLG guidance 3333 recommends that a secure external terminal box (also serving cabling for other services) should be fitted at the cable entry point. The internal entry point should be an equipment cabinet which acts as a distribution point for digital services as well as telephony, satellite and cable TV etc.

Connectivity Within the Home
Equipment within the home may employ a wide range of cabling of both a standard and proprietary type. Some may also connect using a wireless and / or powerline technologies. Both cabling and wireless solutions are evolving and any internal infrastructure will need to offer sufficient capacity and flexibility to meet future requirements.

There are currently four options for the distribution of digital services within the home. Irrespective of the system used each network device will need to have a network adapter, allowing it to communicate through the network.

Ethernet
The most commonly used cable network, using twisted pair copper cable. Ethernet currently provides the fastest and most reliable transmission medium. It can be provided at modest cost (especially when fitted as part of a new build or major refurbishment programme). However, retrofitting into existing homes can be awkward. Signals are delivered to a standard network access (i.e. RJ45) socket, normally mounted on a faceplate.

Types of cable and fibre commonly used in communication networks were summarised in Table 7.1. Currently the optimum solution is likely to use Cat 5e or Cat 6 cable. However, equipment within the dwelling may employ a wide range of cabling of both a standard and proprietary type. Some may also connect using a wireless technology. Both cabling and wireless solutions are evolving and any internal infrastructure will need to offer sufficient capacity and flexibility to meet future

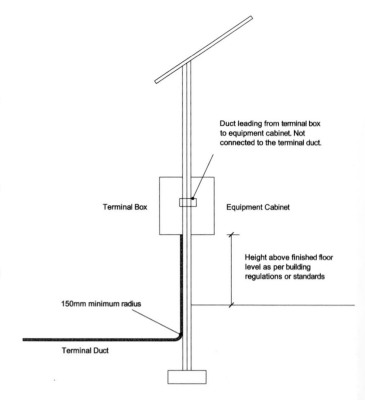

Figure 7.1
Terminal box and equipment cabinet location - CLG Guidance note

requirements.

For digital-capable cabling, current practice is Category 5e (ANSI/TIA/EIA-568-A), or Category 6/6a (ANSI/TIA-568-B.2-1) cable, solid core for up to 100m of installed runs.

The configuration of the cabling installation will depend on the size and nature of the building.

Future-proofing
New cabling standards are likely to be introduced as technology progresses and depending on the intended duration of use of the buildings lifetime before subsequent refurbishment refitting or replacement, some future-proofing may be appropriate. In this case, it would be prudent to lay cabling in an accessible manner, such as in ducting, so that future upgrades may be at minimal cost and disruption.

It is clearly wise to consider the current and foreseeable range of equipment to be installed before deciding which of the currently-available cabling standards to install. There is generally backwards-compatibility built-in to these standards so that fitting a higher grade does not prevent the use of less-demanding equipment.

Ducting
Guidance on ducting infrastructure for new homes is available from the CLG. This guidance does not cover specific cabling requirements. Occupants of dwellings are likely to require:

Data sockets at 'useful locations' throughout the dwelling.

A 'readily accessible' location where network equipment can be installed with a simple 'user-friendly' method of connecting the network equipment to 'live' data sockets.

Mains electricity sockets that are located near the data sockets. The possibility of installing data sockets at 'useful locations' will depend on the nature of the dwellings and the type of occupancy.

However, diverse user needs can only be met by a flexible infrastructure that will allow sockets to be readily installed as and where required. Such a flexible infrastructure would also offer the potential for supporting other cabling distribution requirements. Main and subsidiary ducts should have minimum dimensions to allow for the future expansion of the network.

Ducting should be provided to support the vertical and horizontal distribution of cabling and sockets.

The CLG document does not provide guidance on specific types of ducts. Options that maybe considered include:

Vertical duct concealed with other services in riser.

Ducts in-wall with possibly predefined access and socket positions.

Dado ducting.

Skirting ducting (if not intended for sockets).

Simple surface mounted ducting.

The ducts should be installed such that later cabling, and associated faceplates and sockets, can be installed with minimal disturbance to either previously installed cables or the fabric of the building. The aim should be to facilitate cable installation by an electrician or a qualified competent person. The CLG document does not specify duct sizes but provides the following as guidance (larger ducts should be used where space permits):

Main ducts (that run from the equipment cabinet both vertically and horizontally) should have a minimum cross sectional area of 800mm2, with the smallest dimension being 20mm (i.e. a 20mm x 40mm duct).

Other ducts that spur from main ducts to each room should have a minimum cross sectional area of 400mm2, with the smallest dimension being 20mm (i.e. a 20mm x 20mm duct).

Other recommendations In reference 3 include:

The ducts should enable cables to be installed with a minimum (long term) bending radius of 60mm.

Bends in the ducts should be kept to a minimum. Access points should be provided where there are multiple bends or bends greater than 45 degrees.

Access points to under floor horizontal ducting should remain available through floorboards or other floor components.

The ducts for data services should be separate from main electricity cables and comply with cable separation and routing standards.

Where a vertical duct runs between floors the relevant provisions of the Building Regulations / Standards should be followed, notably with respect to fire safety, resistance to moisture and resistance to sound.

Ducts should be positioned in such a way that damage from 'DIY' is minimised. A similar approach to the best practice installation of electrical cables and sockets should be considered.

The ducts should enable 'standard size' face plates and data sockets to be readily installed.

By removing / cutting a section of ducting to directly insert a

faceplate – using ducting that has ideally been designed for the purpose.

Locating faceplates (with appropriate back boxes) adjacent to accessible ducting.

Data sockets (and other sockets supported by the internal infrastructure) must be located at a height above finished level floor that is in accordance with Building Regulations/Standards. Any data sockets located in the loft area should be located in such a position as not to put the resident at risk from trailing cables etc.

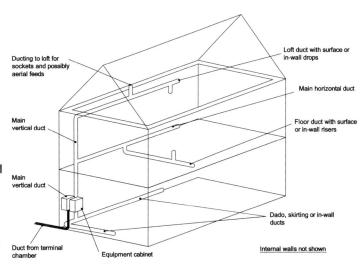

Figure 7.2
Duct distribution in a house - CLG Guidance note

Wireless
This has a number of advantages, especially in existing homes where retrofitting cables may be difficult and expensive. It is easier to install than other current solutions; no additional wiring is required to reach equipment in other parts of the home, and therefore new equipment maybe installed at minimal additional cost. Wireless access points simply need access to power and data (wired or wireless). Devices connected to a wireless network can be located anywhere within the home provided there is sufficient signal reception. New devices can readily be added without having to install new cabling. The most common wireless networks currently in use are Wireless B and Wireless G. However, these are being superseded by Wireless N. Whilst wireless connectivity has many advantages there are disadvantages. Connectivity is affected by location, and obstacles such as the building structure (e.g. conducting metals) and water. They may be susceptible to interference from other devices including portable/mobile telephones and microwave ovens. As the signals may be accessed outside the boundary of the home they may be susceptible to unauthorised access. They should therefore be suitably encrypted to ensure security. Example standards for wireless data include: Wireless Lan ("wifi", IEEE 802.11), Bluetooth, zigbee. Others may be introduced in the future.

Wireless LAN ("wifi") standard is typically IEEE 802.11g or 802.11n at present. Earlier standards 802.11b and 802.11a are slower and offer no significant cost benefits. In general the network is established by a master hub and devices communicate through the hub. The hub will typically be connected via Ethernet on cat 5 or cat 6 cable to a wider network externally, or via ADSL on the home's broadband telephone service.

Bluetooth is an alternative and commonly-used standard. Devices communicate with each other by pairing and no hub is required (therefore no wiring is required). Bandwidth and range are more limited than for wifi, but are typically suitable for many assisted living devices within a room or small flat.

DECT is an established wireless telephone handset standard that is only commonly used for telephone voice services. A DECT basestation is connected like a traditional phone to the external telephone line, and a power socket is required. This standard extends the reach of a telephone to anywhere in a standard dwelling.

Zigbee is a wireless technology standard for low data rate networks based on IEEE 802.15.4-2003. The technology defined by the ZigBee specification is intended to be simpler and less expensive than other WPANs, such as Bluetooth. ZigBee is targeted at radio-frequency (RF) applications that require a low data rate, long battery life, and secure networking. It is suitable for sensors and control devices of building automation systems where small amounts of data are transmitted.

All wireless standards can be susceptible to signal limitations in buildings with thick or metallic walls, or in larger buildings such as residential blocks. Therefore signal-repeaters may be needed to extend the signal into all parts of the building. Wifi performs better than the other standards in this respect.

Phone network
Existing home phone networks can be used as data channels where phone sockets are suitably distributed. As the voice and data signals are transmitted at different frequencies there is not likely to be any interference provided appropriate filters are used.

Powerline
Powerline technologies use mains electricity wiring within the home for the distribution of data. Mains plug adapters link the network devices to the mains electricity cabling. Suitably equipped devices modulate their external data signals onto this network and other suitably-equipped devices receive this data anywhere within the same power distribution. As most existing houses have extensive electric cabling, with power outlets in most rooms, this approach can be widely used. It requires no additional wiring around the home, so new equipment may be installed at minimal additional cost. It is therefore particularly suitable for low-cost and low-disruption refurbishments.

However, there are drawbacks in that they may be susceptible to unauthorised access and may be affected by earthing faults. In retrofit cases, there may be performance limitations depending on the age and quality of the power cabling and installation. In new buildings, such performance limitations should be avoidable by adhering to current standards. There may be considerations of resident alterations to power points that may reduce the performance.

Systems such as HomePlug, Universal Powerline Association, HD-PLC are available which carry data communications over the building's power wiring. IEEE 1901 is a draft standard.

The continued existence of non-interoperable standards presents a risk that equipment may not be supported in the future if standards become obsolete through competition, but equipment installed to an existing standard should remain fully functional within an installation once installed, as long as there is no interference with power point.

Installation costs for cabling will be higher because of both labour and materials, but the benefits may be that more functionality may be obtained at higher reliability than for wireless methods. Powerline methods may offer the best of both worlds, but the

technology is less mature and reliability is reputedly lacking. Once installed, most data networks require little maintenance unless new equipment is introduced, in which case access may be needed to add more capacity or replace lower-capacity equipment. In general maintenance costs could be minimised by ensuring easy access to cabling ducts and equipment housing. Repairs to installations should be considered in the same light.

Training of installation engineers will be higher for cabling methods, especially in refurbishments, since it will involve

	Wired networks			Wired networks
	Ethernet	Phone networks	HomePlug	Wireless-G and Wireless-N
Maximum speed	10/ 100/ 1000Mbps	HPNA 2.0, 128Mbps HPNA 3.0, 240Mbps	HomePlug 1.0, 14Mbps HomePlug AV, 100Mbps	Wireless B: 11Mbps Wireless G: 54Mbps Wireless N: 200+Mbps
Operational speed	4/ 55/ 500-600Mbaps	5 Mbps 60-100Mbps	6 Mbps 30-60Mbps	4-6 Mbps 1 5-40 Mbps 25-60 Mbps 100-125 Mbps
Cost of hardware	Least expensive	Moderate	Moderate	Most expensive at present
Transmission media	Cat 5, Cat 5e or Cat 6 cable with RJ45 connections.	Uses existing phone line installation	Existing AC powerlines	Wireless B Wireless G Wireless N and future developments
Cost of transmission media	Most costly as it requires new cabling	Low if existing phone cabling network is used.	Low if existing power cabling is used	Lowest cost as there are no cable installation costs.
Cost of installation	Most costly as it requires new cabling.	Low if existing phone cabling network is used.	Low if existing power cabling is used.	Lowest cost as there are no cable installation costs.
Pros	Most reliable, highest transmission speed.	Best balance between cost, transmission speed and ease of installation.	Good balance between cost, transmission speed and ease of installation; pre-installed data outlets required in most rooms	Best flexibility for use of laptop, and other network devices. No cable installation is required
Cons	For existing homes, cost of installation can be messy, disruptive and expensive.	Phone connection point must be located close to each network device.	Susceptible to unauthorised access, e.g. from immediate neighbours.	Speed and reliability of signal is affected by building fabric and presence of conducting obstructions. There can be interference from other wireless devices using close transmission bands. Susceptible to unauthorised access.

Table 7.1
Advantages and disadvantages of the four types of data transmission media - BRE

making expert judgements about the best typology in each situation, and require additional building skills. For new buildings this may be less severe. Wireless and powerline installations require less training for the building work itself.

Commissioning of equipment may require skills such as setting up protocols and network communications; however much equipment available today aims to minimise this work at installation through the use of automated set-up. Wifi is particularly troublesome to introduce new equipment particularly when security is enabled; some degree of training is probably needed for this.

When building new residential property, which is designed to last a generation or more, there is a significant expectation of unforeseen technology being introduced during its occupancy. An adequate level of future-proofing would therefore be to install the latest commonly-available cabling (e.g. Cat 6) in ducting. The cost of doing this at build-time should be significantly lower than doing it later. If the building is constructed using steel-reinforced methods, then wireless use may be restricted to within single rooms only, and cabling becomes the most attractive option.

For refurbishing or refitting existing property, the nature and fabric of the building will dictate choices, as will the budget.

For installing equipment and services in existing property while it is in use, minimal disruption is required, or when budgets are restricted, then using wireless or powerline should be considered first, before then considering surface cabling.

The lowest installation costs can be expected with wireless and powerline methods. Installation costs should include the cost of the equipment to be used, in case tradeoffs between equipment and network costs arise: these may depend on market forces and vary from time to time.

Installation costs for cabling will be higher because of both labour and materials, but the benefits may be that more functionality may be obtained at higher reliability than for wireless methods. Powerline methods may offer the best of both worlds, but the technology is less mature and reliability is reputedly lacking.

Once installed, most data networks require little maintenance unless new equipment is introduced, in which case access may be needed to add more capacity or replace lower-capacity equipment. In general maintenance costs could be minimised by ensuring easy access to cabling ducts and equipment housing. Repairs to installations should be considered in the same light. Training of installation engineers will be higher for cabling methods, especially in refurbishments, since it will involve making expert judgements about the best typology in each situation, and require additional building skills. For new buildings this may be less severe. Wireless and powerline installations require less training for the building work itself.

Commissioning of equipment may require skills such as setting up protocols and network communications; however much equipment available today aims to minimise this work at installation through the use of automated set-up. Wifi is particularly troublesome to introduce new equipment particularly when security is enabled; some degree of training is probably needed for this.

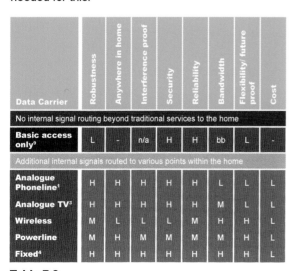

Table 7.2
Options for data infrastructure provision in new buildings - BRE

Data Carrier	Robustness	Anywhere in home	Interference proof	Security	Reliability	Bandwidth	Flexibility/ future proof	Cost
No internal signal routing beyond traditional services to the home								
Basic access only[9]	L	-	n/a	H	H	bb	L	-
Additional internal signals routed to various points within the home								
Analogue Phoneline[1]	H	H	H	H	H	L	L	L
Analogue TV[3]	H	H	H	H	H	M	L	L
Wireless	M	L	L	L	M	H	H	L
Powerline	M	H	M	M	M	M	H	L
Fixed[4]	H	H	H	H	H	H	H	L

1 existing = power and 1 analogue phoneline delivering broadband ADSL to home: no internal communications.

2 e.g. 'Lifeline' distributed around house using analogue twisted pair.

3 e.g. coax cable distribution around house.

4 assuming cat5/ 6 ethernet etc.

nb. L, M and H indicate low, medium and high where high is best.

What is needed in a smart home for different scenarios?
Occupants of dwellings are likely to require:

Access to the network at 'useful locations' throughout the dwelling.

A 'readily accessible' location where network equipment can be installed with a simple 'user-friendly' method of connecting the network equipment to 'live' data sockets.

Conveniently located mains electricity sockets.

The possibility of installing access to the network at 'useful locations' will depend on the nature of the dwellings and the type of occupancy. However, diverse user needs can only be met by a flexible infrastructure that will allow access to be readily achieved as and where required. Such a flexible infrastructure would also offer the potential for supporting other cabling distribution requirements.

Where a cable network is utilised it is important that sufficient data sockets are installed and that they are distributed throughout the home to provide ease of access. Reference 2 states that two double faceplates should be provided per room, located at approximately opposite and accessible locations. Each faceplate should be located close to power sockets. They should be positioned about 1m above floor level to facilitate access and reduce the risk of flood damage. Reference 2 also recommends that a draft layout plan is prepared to facilitate visualising and testing of the proposed layout.

The following table gives examples of the types of services or assisted living solutions that are enabled by the Data Networking methodology adopted.

1 existing = power and 1 analogue phoneline delivering broadband ADSL to home: no internal communications.

2 e.g. 'Lifeline' distributed around house using analogue twisted pair.

Design

Provided that some basic principles are applied and the right things are done, intelligent buildings can bring many benefits to building owners, users and the environment. Regardless of the systems and services incorporated in an intelligent building, it is essential that those responsible for their integration are consulted early in the building's design and construction so that

Data Carrier	Robustness	Anywhere in home	Interference proof	Security	Reliability	Bandwidth	Flexibility/ future proof	Cost
No internal signal routing beyond traditional services to the home								
Basic access only[3]	L	0	n/a	H	H	bb	L	-
Additional internal signals routed to various points within the home								
Analogue Phoneline[1]	H	H	H	H	H	L	L	H
Analogue TV[3]	H	H	H	H	H	M	L	H
Digital: Wireless	M	L	L	L	M	H	H	L
Digital: Powerline	M	H	M	M	M	M	H	L
Digital: Fixed[4]	H	H	H	H	H	H	H	H

Table 7.3
Options for data infrastructure provision in existing buildings through retrofit or refurbishment - BRE

full advantage may be taken of the benefits offered. It would be a considerably more complex and costly process to reconfigure the building's cabling to accommodate additional services once it has been installed, for example. The following should be considered in order to exploit the full potential of an intelligent building:

Planning

e.g. early engagement of designers and the ultimate owner of the communications network to ensure that it will meet both current and future requirements of the building in terms of access and bandwidth, and consideration of how the systems and services to be provided within the building will be integrated.

Flexibility

Example the use of 'open' communications protocols to provide supplier choice, consideration of the way in which changes or additions to the building systems will be accommodated, and how the communications network will accommodate changes in the internal layout or use of the building.

Sustainability

e.g. monitoring and minimising the use energy, water, materials etc.

Management

e.g. responsibility for ensuring that the building is performing as it should, resources and training requirements, how the performance of the building and its systems will be monitored.

Maintenance

e.g. Arranging systems maintenance when required, responsibility for this and associated training needs.

Assessment

The criteria and metrics to be used to assess the performance of the building, responsibilities and implementations of findings.

Differentiation

How the operation of building systems will be combined to provide a safer, more sustainable and user-friendly environment for building users while fulfilling legal and regulatory requirements.

Intelligent building systems can provide an effective means of helping to ensure that buildings and their owners meet relevant legal and regulatory requirements.

New Build and Refurbishment

A dedicated cabled network is likely to be the optimum solution in new build (see Section Guidance currently under development by BIS). Installing cabling in an existing home can be disruptive and expensive. Cabling routes need to fit with the existing structure and may need to be cut into the building fabric or may require access to confined spaces. In major refurbishment programmes it may be economical to install cabling as outlined above for new build. The specific installation may also require high levels of reliability or fast transmission speeds in which case cabling may be the only option. According to reference 2 retrofitting cables should make use of spaces and mounting surfaces in attics, suspended or sleeper floors, built-in storage areas, soffits, basements and garages.

Data network	Switch / control	Voice/ audio	Video	Data
No internal signal routing beyond traditional services to the home				
Existing[1]	single alarm unit	single telephone	single TV reception	-
Additional internal signals routed to various points within the home				
Analogue phoneline[2]	alarms to call centre ('Lifeline')	additional analogue telephones, intercoms, emergency voice equipment	-	distributed "Modem" or ADSL routers
Analogue TV[3]	-	-	CCTV (door camera etc.); multiple TV receivers	-
Digital: Wireless / Digital: Powerline / Digital: Fixed[4]	alarms to call centres; environmental controls; control of mobility aids; control of medical equipment	intercoms, emergency voice, monitoring microphones	monitoring cameras; CCTV (door camera etc.); videoconferencing; IP-TV services	health monitoring; equipment monitoring; environment monitoring;

Table 7.4
Assisted Living solutions enabled by data networking - BRE

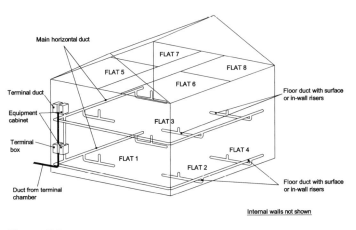

Figure 7.3
Duct distribution in a multi-occupance building - CLG Guidance note

Otherwise wireless, phone network and powerline options can be considered. If a wireless network is selected then the required data socket layout is much simplified as cabling is only needed for the wireless routers. Additional routers or range extenders may be required, however, in large dwellings or where obstacles affect the signal.

Multi-dwelling buildings

The CLG document states that the above guidance for a dwelling house also applies to multi-dwelling buildings such as flats or maisonettes with the following exceptions:

Each dwelling within the building could have a separate equipment cabinet or a cabinet per floor in a public area.

The dwelling ducting from the equipment cabinet should not be routed outside of the dwelling served.

The duct(s) from the terminal chamber should be routed to the equipment cabinets in a common duct with controlled access and restrictions allowing only authorised person's access. The common duct may be routed vertically and / or horizontally.

The common duct should have a minimum cross-sectional area of 2000mm2, with the smallest dimension being 40mm (i.e. a 40mm x 50mm duct). This size should serve up to 15 dwellings but larger ducts should be employed if space permits. The common duct cross sectional area should be increased by 2000mm2 for each additional 15 dwellings.

Where a common duct runs between floors, or horizontally between dwellings, the relevant provisions of the Building Regulations / Standards should be followed. This is especially important with respect to fire safety, resistance to moisture, gas leaks, air tightness and resistance to sound.

At each dwelling the boundary between the external and internal infrastructure should be adjacent to the place where the data service providers' cable may later enter the building. The resident would remain the owner of the ducting that houses the data cable from the service provider. In a multi-dwelling building the boundary between the external and internal infrastructure should be adjacent to the place where the data service providers' cable may later enter the building. The landlord shall therefore have responsibility for a part of the internal infrastructure (including the terminal box and common duct) that may accommodate cables and network equipment that is owned by a data service provider. **Boundaries for ducting between two premises start and end at the dividing wall.**

Cable Routes and Handling

It is important that cables are handled and fixed to meet a number of requirements including:

Minimum bending requirements (for Cat 5e and Cat 6).

Cables must not be kinked.

Cables must be at least a minimum 300mm away from power cables, and must avoid fluorescent lighting control gear and electric motors. Data cables and powerlines should cross at right angles where crossing is necessary.

Minimum hole diameter for a single Cat 5e or Cat 6 cable is 6mm (or 18mm if terminated with an RJ45 connector).

Data cables should be run through ducting of suitable dimensions. Ducting should be installed with draw strings to facilitate pulling through cables. The pulling force should not exceed 85N to avoid damaging the cables. Where cables converge they should be labelled.

Holes in walls and floors should be of adequate size for the cable; grommets may be needed to prevent chaffing. Cable hole diameters will need to be increased where cables converge to allow space for cable harnesses.

Notched stapling guns will enable cable fixing without damaging the cable.

Professional quality crimping tools should be used where cables are to be terminated on site.

Stranded patch cables should not exceed 6m in length.

Ethernet installations should be star wired.

The maximum cable run length for ethernet installations is about 90m.

Single-core cable should be used for network cabling. Multi-strand cables should be used for patch cables.

See Chapter 8 for Sample Guidance.

Wiring guidance and examples

There are several internal infrastructures to provide internet (broadband in most cases) connection and control for devices in a building and house. The type of infrastructure that is required is dependent on the reliability, volume of information and security of data for the required assisted living solution. The following examples show how smart home functionality can be implemented in practice. The cables of each system are routed back to the electronic consumer unit.

Example 1

Figure 7.4 shows the wiring for a home PC network with a broadband internet connection. Each RJ45 socket outlet is connected by a Category 5e cable through a patch panel on the electronic consumer unit to a 4-way hub. The hub can connect up to 4 computers together over an Ethernet network. The patch panel is used to select the 4 socket outlets to which computers are to be connected. (Hubs are available with more than 4 ways if required.) The PC network is connected through a 'router' to the ISDN, ADSL or cable modem connection point in the electronic consumer unit. All four PCs can access the internet simultaneously, sharing the available bandwidth.

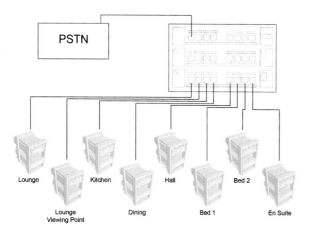

Figure 7.4
PC network with broadband internet connection - Hellerman Tyton

Example 2

Figure 7.5 shows a home PC network with an internet connection linked by cable and radio to household appliances and systems. The connections are made through a 4-way wired hub with an additional radio interface for wireless connections. Again, all the PCs and devices can access the internet simultaneously, sharing the available bandwidth. The home appliance could be a washing machine or gas boiler that is able to report its service status over the internet to the company responsible for its maintenance.

The desktop PCs are shown linked by Category 5e cable to the internal network. The personal digital assistant (PDA) and laptop PC are linked to the network by a wireless IEEE 802.11b connection. The PDA could be used here as a remote control device to operate home appliances or lighting. A mobile telephone with its own internet connection could also be used for this purpose.

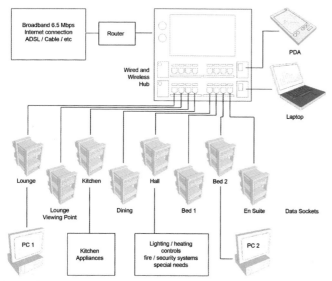

Figure 7.5
Connecting household appliances and systems to the home network - Hellerman Tyton

Example 3

Figure 7.6 shows an example of an 'integrated environmental control system' based on the KNX (formally European Installation Bus - EIB) a standardised control network (which is separate from the PC network). The system can provide flexible control of heating and lighting, as well as security and safety functions. Conventionally heating, lighting and security systems are separate and unable to communicate with each other and share information.

The arrangement in Figure 7.6 allows a passive infrared detector (for example) to signal the presence of an intruder when the house is locked, and to turn on the heating when the house is unlocked and someone enters a room. In a similar way, a window contact can be used to detect a break-in and to turn off the air conditioning if someone opens a window for fresh air.

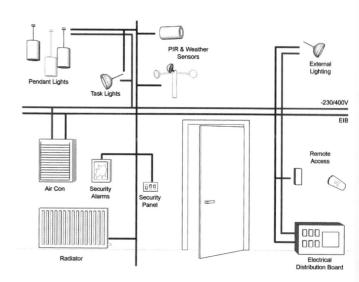

Figure 7.6
Integrated environmental control - BRE

Overall Performance Considerations

These basic performance criteria aim to set the values for implementing solutions for Assisted Living. These criteria cover both the enabling infrastructure and the assisted living solutions that are built on it.

Home based performance:
Solutions must work at any place in the home.

Must work in any home.

Must be immune from interference from other ambient signals (entertainment, phone, communications networks etc.).

Solutions must take account of foreseeable impacts from residents, contractors and other individuals, including common approaches to DIY, wear and tear impact on physical structure, potential for unlawful removal of infrastructure elements or devices, health and safety, maintenance, etc.

Requirement to work in places outside the home is left to ALIP2, as is any requirement to work in another person's home who does not have any installed equipment.

Low Cost
Must aim to minimise the cost of installation and maintenance in existing homes.

Must minimise the disruption to residents during installation and minimise impact on their fabric and fittings through unobtrusive product design and positioning.

Must aim to minimise the cost of installation and maintenance in new homes.

Cost of operation needs to be attractive to all stakeholders.

Future Proofing
Must be capable of altering functionality if an individual's needs change.

Must be upgradeable so that additional features can be added without obsoleting the installation.

Must be capable of adding functionality to keep up with the requirements of service provision enhancements.

Cost of altering functionality must be minimised for all stakeholders.

Environmental
Must take reasonable steps to minimise the power consumption requirements.

Batteries and other consumables should be recyclable where possible.

Equipment that is 10 years or older has an increased potential to fail, and consultation with the manufacturer is critical to determine the upgrade options / replacement path. It was also clear that equipment built to BS7369:1991 the 'original' telecare communication standard does not operate reliably on digital networks, all equipment using this standard must be modified or replaced. (3)

'3'
G. Worsley - Assisted living Innovation Platform - Standards, Interoperability and Broadband.

8. Future Research for Lifehome 21

Future Research for Lifehome 21

At the time of writing advice given by several sources of government supportive documents (PPGs and PPSs), bodies such as CABE are undergoing changes in status.
However the information from these documents enclosed in this document is considered valuable guidance and relevant to assisted living.

Lifehome 21 takes the 16 aspects of Life-Time Homes but adds five extra topics:

WANLANPAN

HUBUGHALL

HOMEOFFICE

GRANATTIC

HOME LIFT: FLUPPER

WANLANPAN
Is a term for (wireless) area networks ranging from Wide to Metropolitan to Local and Personal.

Wide area networks or WAN is a network covering a broad geographical area. Contrast this with personal area networks (PAN's), Local area networks (LAN's) or metropolitan area networks (MAN's). General discussion on these areas is discussed in chapters 6, 7 and in the Introduction.

HUBUGHALL
Is a word for the improved space standards for entrance halls to accommodate working dimensions for buggies and wheelchairs. It is also a possible location for the information hub from which transmission to the rest of the home is either wireless or wired depending on critical health conditions of the occupants. The idea of a hall as not just a vestibule, it is important in architectural terms. See Chapter 3 regarding access that generally indicates a 3m2 increase in the area of halls to accommodate the above.

HOMEOFFICE
Working from home is technically possible for most of workers in the UK. Less able and older people will benefit from workspace provision in homes. However according to research undertaken on behalf of the BCO (British Council for Offices) only 48% of UK employees are offered flexi-time compared with 90% in mainland Europe. (see 'Making Flexible Working Work' by OCCo (Original creative Co-op) and BCO published May 2010.) One of the top five reasons for working from home is that the number of people having caring responsibility for older relatives in the UK is estimated as 10 million in 2010. See also the section on 'family-friendly' employment in 'Getting it Together: The Work-Life Agenda and Offices' by ZZA and UCL, again research undertaken for BCO.

Most people that work from home do not have dedicated space but use a temporary conversion of dining or lounge space to facilitate as office space. Office equipment and additional work space can be better accommodated if an additional 3m2 is added to the Dining or Living spaces shown in the diagrams in Chapter 4.

Tele-Presence Systems suitable for home installations such as CISCO's 'umi' (you me), require symetrical band width and are now available on the market.

GRANATTIC
The Mayor of London's new space standards require that roof space is to be able to be easily convertible to accommodation for the elderly (and others). The Trussed Rafter Association TRA produce guidance on Room in Roof RiR trusses. This guidance may encourage the use of pitched roofs of 40 degrees and over for short span roofs (7m and under).

HOME LIFT: FLUPPER
Flupper is a new form of vertical transportation system to be used within the home. It takes the form and dimensions of a very small lift but is propelled by the user and is a serious alternative to staircases. Several prototypes have been developed by Rombout Frieling at the RCA Innovation and Imperial College. Further research into certification and production are being investigated at BRE and RCA Innovation.

Glossary

24/7 - 24 hours a day, seven days a week. Hence, 24/7 monitoring effectively means continuous monitoring.

Actuator - A device that performs a mechanical action, e.g. opening a valve, in response to an electrical or mechanical input.

Backbone network Connection - In the context of an intelligent building, this defines the part of a communications network that links local area networks or LANs.

Bandwidth - The capacity of a network to transmit data, usually expressed in MHz or GHz. The higher the bandwidth, the greater the capacity of the network to transmit data. Typically, a local area network will have a bandwidth of 100 MHz or more, whereas a backbone network connection will commonly have a bandwidth in excess of 1 GHz.

Building management system - A centralised, often computer-controlled, system for controlling, monitoring and optimizing building systems.

Building systems - The services and functions provided within a building, e.g. lighting, access control, heating.

Closed protocol - A communications protocol, the use of which is restricted to authorised bodies only. Often referred to as a 'proprietary protocol'.

Communications network - A collection of communications links and nodes arranged so that messages may be passed from any part of the network to another, often over multiple links and through various nodes.

Communications protocol - A set of rules defining the format of data communicated between devices – effectively an 'electronic language'.

Gateway - A device that translates data from one communications protocol to another.

GHz - Gigahertz (or 109 Hz). Often used to describe the bandwidth of a communications network.

Integrated systems - Building systems sharing the same communications network.

Interoperability - The ability of devices to replace or work with other devices from different manufacturers without modification using the same communications network – effectively 'plug and play'.

Internet Protocol (IP) - The de facto protocol for communication over the internet.

Local area network (LAN) - A communications network linking systems and devices in a specific area, such as a single floor of a building or a large office.

MHz - Megahertz (or 106 Hz). Often used to describe the bandwidth of a communications network.

Node - A location on a communications network where a device such as a computer or sensor maybe connected.

Open protocol - A communications protocol that is available for general use, although not necessarily royalty free.

Passive Infrared Sensor (PIR sensor) - An electronic device which ommits an infrared beam measuring objects in its field of view. PIR sensors are commonly used as motion detectors triggering external or internal lighting sources for pathways, corridors or stairwells.

Remote monitoring - Monitoring or surveillance performed away from the place at which the monitored activity is occurring. This could be a different room, building, city or country. A typical example is the monitoring of security camera images from multiple sites at a central location.

Request for Comment (RFC) - A document prepared by the Internet Engineering Task Force, which may lead to updates to the way that the internet is operated.

Sensor - A device that responds to a particular stimulus, such as light, temperature or movement, usually by the generation of data that is monitored and controlled by a building management system.

Structured cabling - Involves dividing a communications network into specific subsystems to simplify its design and installation.

Telephony - The electronic communication of the human voice.

Bibliography

Metric Handbook Planning & Design Data (2nd Ed.):
Architectural Press 1999. David Adler.

Neufert Architects' Data (3rd Ed.): Blackwell science,
Ernst and Peter Neufert.

Building Regulations Part K & M.

http://www.fastuk.org/atcommunity/links.php

http://www.direct.gov.uk/en/DisabledPeople/index.htm

http://www.nationwide-mobility.co.uk/ultimate-shower-bath.php/

www.PracticalBathing.co.uk

www.Aquability.com

PremierBathrooms.co.uk

Adjustable worktops
http://www.barrierfree.org/washbasin_accessible_design_01.php
http://www.pressalitcare.com/pressalitcare/en-GB/TheKitchen.
htm

Disabled hoists.
www.jacksonsleisure.co.uk

Homes for the Old Age - CABE .

Lifetime Homes.

Mayor of London GLA Standards.

Code for Sustainable Homes – CLG (Communities & Local
Government Guidance).

Design for Access 2 – Manchester City Council.

Building for Life.org

Design of Accessible Housing – Lifetime Homes.

Universal Design - A Manual and Practicale for Architects
– Architectural Press (2000). Selwyn Goldsmith with PRP
Architects.

Technology Summary page 75 – Paul Rhoades.

Flupper - Rombout Frieling, Royal College of Art 2008_2009.
www.flupper.to

Installing smart home digital networks. Good Building Guide
GBG77 (2009). M Perry.

An Introduction to intelligent buildings: benefits and technology,
BRE Information Paper JP13/08 Part 1 (2008). J Holden.

An Introduction to intelligent buildings: benefits and technology,
BRE Information Paper JP13/08 Part 2 (2008). J Holden.

Assisted Living Inovation Platform (ALIP) - Standards,
Interoperability and Broadband: Graham Worsley

Housing for People with Sight Loss.
A Thomas Pocklington Trust Design Guide (2008).

Wheelchair housing design guide.
Second Edition. BRE Press. 2006. Stephen Thorpe and
Habinteg Housing Trust.

Housing for People with Sight Loss. A Thomas Pocklington Trust
Design Guide. EP 84. IHS BRE Press, 2008. Goodman C.

Wheelchair Housing Design Guide. Second edition. EP 70. IHS
BRE Press, 2006. Thorpe S and Habinteg Housing Association.

Digitally enabled communities. BRE Information Paper 8/10. IHS
BRE Press 2010. Perry M.

Smart home systems and the Code for Sustainable Homes. BRE
Report 506. IHS BRE Press, 2009. Nichols A and Perry M.

> **Birmingham**
12 Caroline Street
Birmingham
B3 1TR
t   +44 (0)121 212 2221
f   +44 (0)121 236 2709

> **Edinburgh**
36 North Castle Street
Edinburgh
EH2 3BN
t   +44 (0)131 225 4040
f   +44 (0)131 225 4747

> **Glasgow**
45 West Nile Street
Glasgow
G1 2PT
t   +44 (0)141 226 3030
f   +44 (0)141 226 3053

> **London**
West End House
11 Hills Place
London
W1F 7SE
t   +44 (0)20 7297 5600
f   +44 (0)20 7297 5601

> **Manchester**
83 Fountain Street
Manchester
M2 2EE
t   +44 (0)161 236 7070
f   +44 (0)161 236 7077

-06.11?

£25.00